DASH Diet Instant Pot Cookbook for Beginners:

150 Low Sodium and Heart Healthy Electric Pressure Cooker Recipes to Lower Blood Pressure

Table of contents

Morning Delights: Breakfast & Brunch

Cinnamon Apple Steel-Cut Oats

Yield: 4 servings | Prep time: 10 minutes | Cook time: 25 minutes

Ingredients:

- 1 cup steel-cut oats
- 2 ½ cups water
- 2 medium apples, cored and chopped
- 1 teaspoon ground cinnamon
- 1 tablespoon pure maple syrup (optional)
- ¼ teaspoon salt (adjust based on DASH Diet requirements)
- 1 teaspoon vanilla extract

Directions:

1. Begin by rinsing the steel-cut oats under cold water for about a minute. This helps in removing excess starch and improving the texture of the cooked oats.
2. Add the rinsed steel-cut oats, water, chopped apples, cinnamon, salt, and maple syrup (if using) to the Instant Pot.
3. Lock the lid of the Instant Pot in place and set the valve to the sealing position. Choose the 'Manual' or 'Pressure Cook' setting and set the timer for 7 minutes on high pressure.
4. Once the cooking time is complete, allow the Instant Pot to naturally release pressure for 15 minutes. After 15 minutes, turn the valve to the venting position to release any remaining pressure.
5. Open the lid, stir in the vanilla extract, and give the oatmeal a good mix.
6. Serve the oatmeal hot. Top with additional fruit or nuts if desired.
7. Store any leftovers in an airtight container in the refrigerator. The oatmeal can be reheated with a little water or milk before serving.

Nutritional Information: 250 calories, 7g protein, 45g carbohydrates, 3.5g fat, 6g fiber, 0mg cholesterol, 80mg sodium, 150mg potassium.

Sunrise Veggie Frittata

Yield: 4 servings | Prep time: 15 minutes | Cook time: 20 minutes

Ingredients:

- 6 large eggs
- 1/4 cup low-fat milk
- 1/2 bell pepper, diced
- 1 small zucchini, diced
- 1/2 medium red onion, finely chopped
- 1 medium tomato, diced
- 1/4 teaspoon black pepper
- 1/4 teaspoon salt (adjust based on DASH Diet requirements)
- 1 tablespoon olive oil
- 1/4 cup chopped fresh parsley

Directions:

1. In a bowl, whisk together eggs, milk, salt, and black pepper. Stir in parsley and set aside.
2. Turn on the Instant Pot to 'Sauté' mode and add olive oil. Once hot, add the bell pepper, zucchini, red onion, and tomato. Sauté for 3-4 minutes, or until vegetables start to soften.
3. Pour the egg mixture over the sautéed vegetables.
4. Lock the lid of the Instant Pot in place, set the valve to the sealing position. Choose the 'Steam' setting and adjust the timer to 10 minutes.
5. Once the cooking time is done, do a quick release. Carefully remove the lid and let the frittata set for a couple of minutes before serving.

Nutritional Information: 180 calories, 12g protein, 8g carbohydrates, 10g fat, 2g fiber, 280mg cholesterol, 200mg sodium, 350mg potassium.

Quinoa Berry Breakfast Bowl

Yield: 4 servings | Prep time: 5 minutes | Cook time: 15 minutes

Ingredients:

- 1 cup quinoa, rinsed and drained
- 2 cups water
- 1/4 teaspoon salt (adjust based on DASH Diet requirements)
- 1 teaspoon vanilla extract
- 2 tablespoons pure maple syrup (optional)
- 1 cup mixed berries (strawberries, blueberries, raspberries)
- 1/4 cup chopped nuts (like almonds or walnuts)
- 1/2 cup low-fat Greek yogurt
- Zest of 1 lemon

Directions:

1. Combine quinoa, water, and salt in the Instant Pot. Secure the lid and set the valve to sealing position. Use the 'Manual' or 'Pressure Cook' setting on high for 1 minute.
2. Once done, allow the Instant Pot to naturally release pressure for 12 minutes, then turn the valve to the venting position to release any remaining pressure.
3. Fluff the quinoa with a fork and stir in the vanilla extract and maple syrup if using.
4. Serve quinoa in bowls, topped with Greek yogurt, mixed berries, chopped nuts, and a sprinkle of lemon zest.

Nutritional Information: 280 calories, 10g protein, 45g carbohydrates, 6g fat, 5g fiber, 3mg cholesterol, 150mg sodium, 320mg potassium.

Whole Grain French Toast Casserole

Yield: 4 servings | Prep time: 20 minutes | Cook time: 25 minutes

Ingredients:

- 6 slices of whole grain bread, cubed
- 4 large eggs
- 1 cup low-fat milk
- 1 teaspoon vanilla extract
- 1/4 teaspoon ground cinnamon
- 1/4 teaspoon salt (adjust based on DASH Diet requirements)
- 2 tablespoons pure maple syrup (optional)
- 1/2 cup mixed berries (like blueberries and raspberries)
- 1/4 cup chopped nuts (like almonds or walnuts, optional)
- 1 tablespoon unsalted butter or coconut oil for greasing

Directions:

1. In a bowl, whisk together eggs, milk, vanilla extract, cinnamon, salt, and maple syrup (if using) until well combined.
2. Add cubed bread into the mixture and gently stir, ensuring all pieces are soaked. Allow the bread to sit in the mixture for about 10 minutes.
3. Grease the bottom of a round baking dish that fits inside your Instant Pot with butter or coconut oil. Transfer the soaked bread mixture into this dish. Sprinkle with berries and nuts.
4. Add 1 cup of water to the Instant Pot. Place the trivet inside and then place the baking dish on top. Close the lid, set the valve to sealing, and cook on 'Manual' or 'Pressure Cook' high for 25 minutes.
5. Once done, let the Instant Pot release pressure naturally for 10 minutes, then turn the valve to venting to release any remaining pressure.

Nutritional Information: 320 calories, 12g protein, 45g carbohydrates, 9g fat, 6g fiber, 185mg cholesterol, 320mg sodium, 290mg potassium.

Spinach & Feta Egg Bake

Yield: 4 servings | Prep time: 10 minutes | Cook time: 20 minutes

Ingredients:

- 6 large eggs
- 1/4 cup low-fat milk
- 2 cups fresh spinach, roughly chopped
- 1/2 cup feta cheese, crumbled
- 1/4 teaspoon black pepper
- 1/4 teaspoon salt (adjust based on DASH Diet requirements)
- 1 small red onion, finely chopped
- 1 tablespoon olive oil
- 1 garlic clove, minced

Directions:

1. In a bowl, whisk together eggs, milk, salt, and black pepper. Add in the feta cheese and set aside.
2. Turn on the Instant Pot to 'Sauté' mode. Add olive oil. Once hot, sauté the red onion until translucent. Add garlic and spinach, sautéing until spinach is wilted.
3. Pour the egg mixture over the sautéed veggies in the pot.
4. Lock the lid, set the valve to sealing. Use the 'Manual' or 'Pressure Cook' setting and adjust the timer to 5 minutes on high.
5. Once done, allow a natural pressure release for 10 minutes, then turn the valve to venting to release any remaining pressure.

Nutritional Information:

200 calories, 13g protein, 6g carbohydrates, 13g fat, 1g fiber, 320mg cholesterol, 400mg sodium, 290mg potassium.

Creamy Polenta with Mixed Berries

Yield: 4 servings | Prep time: 5 minutes | Cook time: 20 minutes

Ingredients:

- 1 cup polenta (cornmeal)
- 4 cups water
- 1/4 teaspoon salt (adjust based on DASH Diet requirements)
- 1 tablespoon olive oil or unsalted butter
- 1/2 cup low-fat milk or almond milk
- 1 tablespoon pure maple syrup (optional)
- 1 cup mixed berries (like blueberries, raspberries, strawberries)
- Fresh mint for garnish (optional)

Directions:

1. In the Instant Pot, combine polenta, water, salt, and olive oil or butter.
2. Lock the lid, set the valve to sealing. Use the 'Porridge' or 'Manual' setting and adjust the timer to 20 minutes on low pressure.
3. Once done, do a quick release of pressure by turning the valve to venting.
4. Stir in the milk until the polenta reaches a creamy consistency. Add maple syrup if desired.
5. Serve hot in bowls, topped with mixed berries and garnished with fresh mint leaves.

Nutritional Information:230 calories, 5g protein, 48g carbohydrates, 4g fat, 3g fiber, 5mg cholesterol, 160mg sodium, 220mg potassium.

Sweet Potato & Black Bean Breakfast Burrito

Yield: 4 servings | Prep time: 15 minutes | Cook time: 20 minutes

Ingredients:

- 2 medium sweet potatoes, peeled and diced
- 1 cup black beans, rinsed and drained
- 1/2 cup fresh salsa (low sodium)
- 1/4 teaspoon ground cumin
- 1/4 teaspoon smoked paprika
- 4 whole grain tortillas
- 1/2 cup low-fat cheese, shredded (optional)
- 1 tablespoon olive oil
- Salt (adjusted for DASH Diet requirements) and pepper to taste
- Fresh cilantro, chopped for garnish
- 1/2 lime, juiced

Directions:

1. Turn the Instant Pot on 'Sauté' mode. Add the olive oil. Once hot, add the sweet potatoes and sauté until slightly browned, about 5 minutes.
2. Add the black beans, ground cumin, smoked paprika, and salsa. Mix well.
3. Close the Instant Pot lid and set to 'Manual' or 'Pressure Cook' on high for 5 minutes. Once done, do a quick release.
4. As the filling cools slightly, warm the tortillas. Spoon a generous portion of the sweet potato and black bean mixture onto each tortilla, sprinkle with cheese if desired, and roll into a burrito. Finish with a splash of lime juice and fresh cilantro.
5. Serve warm.

Nutritional Information:310 calories, 12g protein, 58g carbohydrates, 5g fat, 10g fiber, 5mg cholesterol, 320mg sodium, 720mg potassium.

Mango & Chia Seed Pudding

Yield: 4 servings | Prep time: 10 minutes | Cook time: 5 minutes (primarily for heating, not pressure cooking)

Ingredients:

- 2 cups unsweetened almond milk or low-fat milk
- 1/2 cup chia seeds
- 1 ripe mango, peeled, pitted, and diced
- 2 tablespoons pure maple syrup or honey (adjust for sweetness preference)
- 1 teaspoon pure vanilla extract
- Pinch of salt (adjust based on DASH Diet requirements)

Directions:

1. In a mixing bowl, combine chia seeds, maple syrup (or honey), vanilla extract, and salt.
2. In the Instant Pot, heat the milk using the 'Sauté' function just until it's warm to the touch.
3. Pour the warm milk over the chia seed mixture and stir well to combine.
4. Allow the mixture to sit for about 5 minutes, then give another good stir to prevent any lumps from forming. Let it sit for another 15-20 minutes, occasionally stirring, until it thickens to a pudding-like consistency.
5. Spoon the pudding into bowls or glasses and top with diced mango. Chill for an hour before serving, or enjoy immediately if you prefer a slightly warm pudding.

Nutritional Information:190 calories, 6g protein, 30g carbohydrates, 7g fat, 10g fiber, 0mg cholesterol, 85mg sodium, 300mg potassium.

Vegetable and Cheese Strata

Yield: 4 servings | Prep time: 15 minutes | Cook time: 25 minutes

Ingredients:

- 4 cups whole grain bread, cubed
- 1 cup mixed vegetables (such as bell peppers, zucchini, and spinach), chopped
- 1 cup low-fat cheese, shredded (choose cheeses like cheddar, mozzarella, or feta)
- 4 large eggs
- 1 cup low-fat milk
- 1/4 teaspoon black pepper
- 1/4 teaspoon salt (adjusted for DASH Diet requirements)
- 1/2 teaspoon dried oregano
- 1/2 teaspoon dried basil
- 1 tablespoon olive oil

Directions:

1. In a large bowl, whisk together eggs, milk, salt, black pepper, oregano, and basil.
2. Add the bread cubes to the bowl, pressing them down so they soak up the egg mixture. Allow to sit for about 10 minutes.
3. While the bread is soaking, turn on the Instant Pot's 'Sauté' function and add olive oil. Once hot, add the mixed vegetables and sauté for 5 minutes or until slightly softened.
4. Stir in the soaked bread mixture and half of the shredded cheese. Top with the remaining cheese.
5. Set the Instant Pot to 'Manual' or 'Pressure Cook' on low pressure for 20 minutes. Once done, do a quick release.

Nutritional Information: 295 calories, 19g protein, 33g carbohydrates, 10g fat, 6g fiber, 185mg cholesterol, 490mg sodium, 370mg potassium.

Banana Nut Bread Pudding

Yield: 4 servings | Prep time: 15 minutes | Cook time: 25 minutes

Ingredients:

- 4 cups whole grain bread, cubed
- 2 ripe bananas, mashed
- 1/4 cup walnuts, chopped
- 2 large eggs
- 1 1/2 cups low-fat milk
- 2 tablespoons honey or maple syrup (adjust for sweetness preference)
- 1 teaspoon pure vanilla extract
- 1/2 teaspoon ground cinnamon
- Pinch of salt (adjusted for DASH Diet requirements)
- 1 tablespoon unsalted butter, melted

Directions:

1. In a large bowl, whisk together eggs, milk, honey or maple syrup, vanilla extract, cinnamon, and salt.
2. Add the bread cubes, mashed bananas, and chopped walnuts to the bowl. Gently mix until the bread absorbs the liquid.
3. Grease the inner pot of the Instant Pot with melted butter. Transfer the bread and banana mixture into the pot, ensuring it's evenly distributed.
4. Set the Instant Pot to 'Manual' or 'Pressure Cook' on low pressure for 25 minutes. Once done, allow for a natural release for 10 minutes, then perform a quick release.
5. Serve warm, optionally drizzling with a touch more honey or maple syrup if desired.

Nutritional Information: 330 calories, 12g protein, 52g carbohydrates, 9g fat, 7g fiber, 95mg cholesterol, 260mg sodium, 470mg potassium.

Mediterranean Breakfast Tofu Scramble

Yield: 4 servings | Prep time: 10 minutes | Cook time: 5 minutes

Ingredients:

- 14 oz firm tofu, drained and crumbled
- 1 tablespoon olive oil
- 1 small red onion, diced
- 1 bell pepper, diced (any color)
- 1/2 cup cherry tomatoes, halved
- 1/4 cup Kalamata olives, pitted and sliced
- 1/4 cup crumbled feta cheese (optional for vegan diet)
- 2 tablespoons fresh parsley, chopped
- 1/2 teaspoon turmeric (for color)
- 1 teaspoon dried oregano
- Pinch of black pepper
- 1/4 cup water

Directions:

1. Turn on the Instant Pot on the 'Sauté' setting. Add olive oil, diced onion, and bell pepper. Sauté for 2-3 minutes or until they begin to soften.
2. Add the crumbled tofu, cherry tomatoes, Kalamata olives, turmeric, dried oregano, and black pepper. Stir well, ensuring the turmeric colors the tofu evenly.
3. Pour in the water, then close the lid and set the Instant Pot to 'Manual' or 'Pressure Cook' for 2 minutes.
4. Once the cooking is complete, quick release the pressure. Stir in the feta cheese (if using) and fresh parsley.
5. Serve warm and enjoy!

Nutritional Information: 220 calories, 14g protein, 12g carbohydrates, 14g fat, 4g fiber, 15mg cholesterol, 320mg sodium, 320mg potassium.

Pumpkin Pie Oatmeal

Yield: 4 servings | Prep time: 5 minutes | Cook time: 8 minutes

Ingredients:

- 1 cup steel-cut oats
- 2 1/2 cups water
- 1 cup pumpkin puree (not pumpkin pie filling)
- 2 teaspoons pumpkin pie spice
- 1 tablespoon maple syrup (or to taste)
- 1/4 teaspoon salt
- 1/4 cup chopped pecans (optional)
- 1/4 cup almond milk (or any milk of choice)

Directions:

1. In the Instant Pot, combine steel-cut oats, water, pumpkin puree, pumpkin pie spice, maple syrup, and salt.
2. Secure the lid, set the valve to sealing, and select the 'Porridge' or 'Manual' setting for 8 minutes.
3. Once cooking is complete, allow the Instant Pot to naturally release for 10 minutes, then carefully turn the valve to venting.
4. Open the lid, stir in almond milk, and top with chopped pecans if desired.
5. Serve warm.

Nutritional Information: 260 calories, 8g protein, 45g carbohydrates, 6g fat, 7g fiber, 0mg cholesterol, 80mg sodium, 300mg potassium.

Berry Almond Breakfast Quinoa

Yield: 4 servings | Prep time: 5 minutes | Cook time: 12 minutes

Ingredients:

- 1 cup quinoa, rinsed and drained
- 2 cups water
- 1/2 cup fresh mixed berries (like blueberries, raspberries, and strawberries)
- 1/4 cup slivered almonds
- 1 tablespoon honey or maple syrup (adjust based on sweetness preference)
- 1/2 teaspoon vanilla extract
- A pinch of salt
- 1/4 cup almond milk (or milk of your choice)

Directions:

1. Add quinoa, water, and a pinch of salt to the Instant Pot.
2. Secure the lid, set the valve to sealing, and select the 'Manual' or 'Pressure Cook' setting for 12 minutes.
3. When the cooking cycle is complete, allow the Instant Pot to naturally release for 10 minutes, then turn the valve to venting to release any remaining pressure.
4. Open the lid, fluff the quinoa with a fork, and stir in the honey (or maple syrup), vanilla extract, and almond milk until well combined.
5. Serve in bowls, topped with mixed berries and slivered almonds.

Nutritional Information:250 calories, 8g protein, 40g carbohydrates, 6g fat, 5g fiber, 0mg cholesterol, 60mg sodium, 300mg potassium.

Huevos Rancheros

Yield: 4 servings | Prep time: 10 minutes | Cook time: 8 minutes

Ingredients:

- 1 cup no-salt-added canned black beans, rinsed and drained
- 1 cup diced tomatoes (fresh or no-salt-added canned)
- 4 large eggs
- 4 small whole grain or corn tortillas
- 1/2 cup diced bell peppers (red, green, or a mix)
- 1/4 cup chopped fresh cilantro
- 1/2 teaspoon ground cumin
- 1/4 teaspoon chili powder
- 1/4 teaspoon black pepper
- 1/4 cup low-fat cheese (cheddar or Monterey Jack)
- 1/4 cup diced avocado (for garnish)
- Sliced green onions (for garnish)

Directions:

1. In the Instant Pot, combine black beans, diced tomatoes, bell peppers, ground cumin, chili powder, and black pepper. Mix thoroughly.
2. Create four wells in the bean-tomato mixture and carefully crack an egg into each well.
3. Secure the lid, set the valve to sealing, and use the 'Manual' or 'Pressure Cook' setting for 3 minutes (for runny yolks) or 5 minutes (for firmer yolks).
4. Once the cooking cycle is complete, perform a quick release by turning the valve to venting.
5. Serve the egg and bean mixture on a tortilla, sprinkled with cheese, cilantro, avocado, and green onions.

Nutritional Information:275 calories, 15g protein, 32g carbohydrates, 10g fat, 8g fiber, 185mg cholesterol, 200mg sodium, 500mg potassium.

Sausage & Pepper Breakfast Casserole

Yield: 4 servings | Prep time: 15 minutes | Cook time: 25 minutes

Ingredients:

- 8 oz turkey sausage, removed from casings and crumbled
- 1 red bell pepper, diced
- 1 green bell pepper, diced
- 4 large eggs
- 1/4 cup skim milk
- 1 cup cubed whole grain bread
- 1/4 teaspoon black pepper
- 1/4 teaspoon dried oregano
- 1/4 cup shredded low-sodium, low-fat cheese (e.g., mozzarella)
- 1/4 cup chopped fresh parsley (for garnish)

Directions:

1. Set the Instant Pot to the 'Sauté' mode. Add the crumbled turkey sausage and cook until browned, then add the diced bell peppers and cook until they soften.
2. In a separate bowl, whisk together the eggs, skim milk, black pepper, and oregano. Stir in the cubed bread ensuring each piece is well-coated with the egg mixture.
3. Turn off the 'Sauté' mode, add the bread and egg mixture to the Instant Pot, and mix well with the sausage and peppers.
4. Secure the lid, set the valve to sealing, and select 'Manual' or 'Pressure Cook' setting for 20 minutes.
5. Once the cooking cycle is complete, perform a quick release by turning the valve to venting. Sprinkle the casserole with cheese and let it melt from the residual heat. Garnish with fresh parsley before serving.

Nutritional Information: 280 calories, 19g protein, 21g carbohydrates, 11g fat, 3g fiber, 195mg cholesterol, 380mg sodium, 350mg potassium.

Heart-Healthy Soups & Stews

Tuscan White Bean Soup

Yield: 4 servings | Prep time: 15 minutes | Cook time: 25 minutes

Ingredients:

- 2 tbsp olive oil
- 1 medium onion, finely chopped
- 2 garlic cloves, minced
- 2 celery stalks, diced
- 2 carrots, diced
- 4 cups low-sodium vegetable broth

- 2 cans (15 oz each) white beans (like cannellini), rinsed and drained
- 1 tsp dried rosemary
- 1/4 tsp black pepper
- 2 cups chopped kale or spinach
- 1 tbsp lemon juice
- Grated Parmesan cheese for garnish (optional, and ensure it's low sodium)

Directions:

1. Select the 'Sauté' mode on the Instant Pot. Add olive oil, onion, garlic, celery, and carrots. Sauté until the onions are translucent.
2. Add vegetable broth, white beans, rosemary, and black pepper. Mix well.
3. Lock the lid in place and set the valve to sealing. Choose 'Manual' or 'Pressure Cook' for 20 minutes.
4. After cooking, use the quick release method. Stir in the kale or spinach, letting it wilt from the residual heat. Mix in the lemon juice.
5. Serve hot, garnished with grated Parmesan if desired.

Nutritional Information:

240 calories, 13g protein, 41g carbohydrates, 5g fat, 10g fiber, 0mg cholesterol, 280mg sodium, 790mg potassium.

Butternut Squash & Apple Soup

Yield: 4 servings | Prep time: 15 minutes | Cook time: 20 minutes

Ingredients:

- 1 medium butternut squash, peeled, seeded, and diced
- 2 medium apples, peeled, cored, and chopped (preferably tart varieties like Granny Smith)
- 1 medium onion, chopped
- 2 cloves garlic, minced
- 1 tbsp olive oil

- 4 cups low-sodium vegetable broth
- 1/2 tsp ground cinnamon
- 1/4 tsp ground nutmeg
- 1/4 tsp black pepper
- 1/4 cup unsweetened almond milk (or other non-dairy milk)
- Salt, to taste (optional)

Directions:

1. Select the 'Sauté' mode on the Instant Pot. Add olive oil, onions, and garlic. Sauté until the onions are translucent.
2. Add the butternut squash, apples, vegetable broth, cinnamon, nutmeg, and black pepper. Stir to combine.
3. Secure the lid, set the valve to sealing, and select 'Manual' or 'Pressure Cook' for 15 minutes.
4. Once done, use the quick release method. Blend the soup using an immersion blender or carefully transfer to a regular blender.
5. Stir in the almond milk, adjust seasoning if needed, and serve hot.

Nutritional Information: 180 calories, 2g protein, 45g carbohydrates, 3g fat, 7g fiber, 0mg cholesterol, 130mg sodium, 700mg potassium.

Chicken Barley Soup

Yield: 4 servings | Prep time: 20 minutes | Cook time: 25 minutes

Ingredients:

- 2 boneless, skinless chicken breasts, cut into bite-sized pieces
- 1 cup pearl barley, rinsed
- 1 medium onion, chopped
- 2 carrots, peeled and sliced
- 2 celery stalks, chopped
- 4 cups low-sodium chicken broth
- 2 cups water
- 2 cloves garlic, minced
- 1 tbsp olive oil
- 1/2 tsp dried thyme
- 1/2 tsp dried rosemary
- Salt and pepper, to taste (be moderate with salt for DASH suitability)
- Fresh parsley, chopped (for garnish, optional)

Directions:

1. Select the 'Sauté' mode on the Instant Pot. Add olive oil, onion, carrots, celery, and garlic. Sauté until the vegetables are slightly softened.
2. Add the chicken pieces to the pot and lightly brown on all sides.
3. Add the barley, chicken broth, water, thyme, and rosemary. Stir to combine.
4. Secure the lid, set the valve to sealing, and select 'Manual' or 'Pressure Cook' for 20 minutes.
5. Once done, use the quick release method. Adjust seasoning, garnish with fresh parsley if desired, and serve hot.

Nutritional Information:220 calories, 20g protein, 30g carbohydrates, 3g fat, 6g fiber, 45mg cholesterol, 150mg sodium, 550mg potassium.

Lentil & Vegetable Stew

Yield: 4 servings | Prep time: 15 minutes | Cook time: 25 minutes

Ingredients:

- 1 cup dried green lentils, rinsed and drained
- 1 medium onion, chopped
- 2 carrots, peeled and diced
- 2 celery stalks, chopped
- 1 bell pepper, chopped
- 2 cloves garlic, minced
- 4 cups low-sodium vegetable broth
- 1 cup diced tomatoes (canned or fresh)
- 1 tsp dried thyme
- 1 tsp dried rosemary
- 2 tbsp olive oil
- Salt and pepper, to taste (be moderate with salt for DASH suitability)
- 1 cup chopped kale or spinach
- 1 zucchini, chopped
- Fresh parsley, chopped (for garnish, optional)

Directions:

1. Using the 'Sauté' mode on the Instant Pot, heat olive oil and add onion, carrots, celery, bell pepper, and garlic. Sauté until the vegetables start to soften.
2. Add lentils, vegetable broth, diced tomatoes, thyme, rosemary, zucchini, and kale or spinach. Stir to combine.
3. Secure the lid, set the valve to sealing, and select 'Manual' or 'Pressure Cook' for 18 minutes.
4. Once the cooking cycle is complete, use the natural release method for 10 minutes, followed by the quick release.
5. Adjust seasoning, garnish with fresh parsley if desired, and serve hot.

Nutritional Information:210 calories, 12g protein, 35g carbohydrates, 4g fat, 12g fiber, 0mg cholesterol, 180mg sodium, 700mg potassium.

Spiced Pumpkin Soup

Yield: 4 servings | Prep time: 10 minutes | Cook time: 15 minutes

Ingredients:

- 4 cups pumpkin puree (fresh or canned)
- 1 medium onion, chopped
- 2 cloves garlic, minced
- 4 cups low-sodium vegetable broth
- 1 tsp ground cinnamon
- 1/2 tsp ground nutmeg
- 1/4 tsp ground ginger
- 2 tbsp olive oil
- Salt and pepper, to taste (use sparingly for DASH suitability)
- 1/2 cup light coconut milk
- Fresh parsley or chives for garnish (optional)

Directions:

1. Set the Instant Pot to 'Sauté' mode and heat olive oil. Add onions and garlic, sautéing until translucent.
2. Add pumpkin puree, vegetable broth, cinnamon, nutmeg, and ginger to the pot. Stir well to combine.
3. Secure the lid, set the valve to sealing, and select 'Manual' or 'Pressure Cook' for 10 minutes.
4. Once the cooking cycle is complete, use the natural release method for 5 minutes, then perform a quick release.
5. Stir in coconut milk, adjust seasoning, garnish if desired, and serve hot.

Nutritional Information: 165 calories, 3g protein, 30g carbohydrates, 5g fat, 7g fiber, 0mg cholesterol, 120mg sodium, 400mg potassium.

Moroccan Chickpea Stew

Yield: 4 servings | Prep time: 15 minutes | Cook time: 20 minutes

Ingredients:

- 2 cups dried chickpeas, soaked overnight and drained
- 1 large onion, chopped
- 2 cloves garlic, minced
- 2 large tomatoes, diced
- 2 carrots, sliced
- 1 bell pepper, diced (red or yellow)
- 3 cups low-sodium vegetable broth
- 2 tsp ground cumin
- 2 tsp ground coriander
- 1 tsp ground turmeric
- 1/2 tsp ground cinnamon
- 2 tbsp olive oil
- 1/4 cup fresh cilantro, chopped
- Salt and pepper to taste (use sparingly for DASH suitability)
- 1 lemon, juiced

Directions:

1. Set the Instant Pot to 'Sauté' mode. Add olive oil, onions, and garlic, sautéing until translucent.
2. Add the spices (cumin, coriander, turmeric, and cinnamon) to the pot and stir for a minute until aromatic.
3. Add the soaked chickpeas, tomatoes, carrots, bell pepper, and vegetable broth. Stir to combine.
4. Secure the lid, set the valve to sealing, and select 'Manual' or 'Pressure Cook' for 15 minutes.
5. Once done, use the quick release method. Stir in fresh cilantro and lemon juice. Adjust seasoning if necessary before serving.

Nutritional Information: 275 calories, 12g protein, 45g carbohydrates, 7g fat, 12g fiber, 0mg cholesterol, 150mg sodium, 600mg potassium.

Beef & Vegetable Minestrone

Yield: 4 servings | Prep time: 20 minutes | Cook time: 30 minutes

Ingredients:

- 1/2 lb lean beef stew meat, cut into bite-sized pieces
- 2 tbsp olive oil
- 1 onion, diced
- 2 cloves garlic, minced
- 2 carrots, sliced
- 2 celery stalks, chopped
- 1 zucchini, diced
- 1 cup green beans, trimmed and cut into 1-inch lengths
- 1 can (14 oz) low-sodium diced tomatoes
- 4 cups low-sodium beef broth
- 1/2 cup whole grain pasta (e.g., fusilli or penne)
- 1 tsp dried oregano
- 1 tsp dried basil
- 1 bay leaf
- Salt and pepper to taste (use sparingly for DASH suitability)
- 1/4 cup fresh parsley, chopped
- 1/4 cup grated Parmesan cheese (optional for serving)

Directions:

1. Set the Instant Pot to 'Sauté' mode. Add olive oil. Once hot, add the beef pieces and brown on all sides. Remove and set aside.
2. In the same pot, add onions, garlic, carrots, and celery, sautéing until the onions become translucent.
3. Add the zucchini, green beans, diced tomatoes, beef broth, oregano, basil, and bay leaf. Return the browned beef to the pot.
4. Secure the lid, set the valve to sealing, and select 'Manual' or 'Pressure Cook' for 20 minutes.
5. Once done, use the quick release method. Stir in pasta and let sit for about 8-10 minutes until pasta is cooked. Before serving, stir in fresh parsley and adjust seasoning if necessary.

Nutritional Information: 310 calories, 24g protein, 27g carbohydrates, 10g fat, 5g fiber, 45mg cholesterol, 280mg sodium, 680mg potassium.

Creamy Broccoli & Spinach Soup

Yield: 4 servings | Prep time: 15 minutes | Cook time: 20 minutes

Ingredients:

- 2 tbsp olive oil
- 1 onion, chopped
- 3 cloves garlic, minced
- 4 cups broccoli florets
- 2 cups fresh spinach, roughly chopped
- 4 cups low-sodium vegetable broth
- 1 cup unsweetened almond milk
- Salt and pepper to taste (use sparingly for DASH suitability)
- 1/4 cup nutritional yeast (or grated Parmesan for non-vegan option)
- 1/2 tsp nutmeg
- 1 tbsp lemon juice
- Fresh parsley for garnish

Directions:

1. Set the Instant Pot to 'Sauté' mode. Add olive oil, onion, and garlic. Sauté until onions become translucent.
2. Add broccoli florets and sauté for another 3 minutes. Then add the spinach, stirring until it wilts.
3. Pour in the vegetable broth and almond milk. Add nutmeg, salt, and pepper.
4. Secure the lid, set the valve to sealing, and select 'Manual' or 'Pressure Cook' for 7 minutes. Once done, use the quick release method.
5. Using an immersion blender, blend the soup until creamy. Stir in lemon juice and nutritional yeast. Serve hot, garnished with fresh parsley.

Nutritional Information: 180 calories, 8g protein, 20g carbohydrates, 8g fat, 6g fiber, 0mg cholesterol, 280mg sodium, 520mg potassium.

Hearty Mushroom & Barley Soup

Yield: 4 servings | Prep time: 15 minutes | Cook time: 25 minutes

Ingredients:

- 1 tbsp olive oil
- 1 onion, diced
- 2 cloves garlic, minced
- 2 cups assorted mushrooms (like cremini, shiitake, and portobello), sliced
- 3/4 cup pearl barley, rinsed
- 5 cups low-sodium vegetable broth
- 2 carrots, diced
- 2 celery stalks, diced
- 1 tsp dried thyme
- 1 bay leaf
- Salt and pepper to taste (use sparingly for DASH suitability)
- 2 tbsp fresh parsley, chopped (for garnish)

Directions:

1. Set the Instant Pot to 'Sauté' mode. Add olive oil, onion, garlic, and mushrooms. Sauté until mushrooms release their moisture and onions become translucent.
2. Add barley, carrots, celery, thyme, bay leaf, and vegetable broth to the pot. Season with a small pinch of salt and pepper.
3. Secure the lid, set the valve to sealing, and select 'Manual' or 'Pressure Cook' for 18 minutes. Once done, allow for a natural pressure release for 5 minutes, then use the quick release method.
4. Remove the bay leaf, give the soup a good stir, and adjust seasonings if needed. Serve hot, garnished with fresh parsley.

Nutritional Information: 210 calories, 6g protein, 42g carbohydrates, 3g fat, 9g fiber, 0mg cholesterol, 240mg sodium, 420mg potassium.

Chicken Pho

Yield: 4 servings | Prep time: 20 minutes | Cook time: 45 minutes

Ingredients:

- 1 lb boneless, skinless chicken breasts
- 1 onion, peeled and halved
- 3-inch piece of fresh ginger, halved lengthwise
- 5 cups low-sodium chicken broth
- 2 star anise pods
- 1 cinnamon stick
- 2 tsp coriander seeds
- 2 tsp fennel seeds
- 3 tbsp fish sauce (low sodium if available)
- 8 oz rice noodles
- Toppings: Fresh bean sprouts, sliced jalapeños, fresh cilantro, lime wedges, and Thai basil (optional)
- Salt to taste (use sparingly for DASH suitability)

Directions:

1. Set the Instant Pot to 'Sauté' mode. Add the onion and ginger, cut side down, and cook without stirring until they begin to char, about 4 minutes.
2. Add star anise, cinnamon, coriander, and fennel to the pot and toast lightly for 1-2 minutes.
3. Add chicken, chicken broth, and fish sauce to the pot. Secure the lid, set the valve to sealing, and select 'Manual' or 'Pressure Cook' for 15 minutes. Allow for a natural pressure release after.
4. While the chicken cooks, prepare rice noodles as per the package instructions. Set aside.
5. Once the Instant Pot's pressure is fully released, open the lid and remove the chicken. Shred it and return to the pot. Season with a small pinch of salt if needed. Serve hot over rice noodles with desired toppings.

Nutritional Information: 300 calories, 28g protein, 32g carbohydrates, 4g fat, 2g fiber, 65mg cholesterol, 520mg sodium, 450mg potassium.

Spicy Sweet Potato & Lentil Soup

Yield: 4 servings | Prep time: 15 minutes | Cook time: 30 minutes

Ingredients:

- 2 medium-sized sweet potatoes, peeled and cubed
- 1 cup dried lentils, rinsed and drained
- 1 onion, diced
- 3 garlic cloves, minced
- 1 red bell pepper, diced
- 5 cups low-sodium vegetable broth
- 1 tsp ground cumin
- 1/2 tsp smoked paprika
- 1/2 tsp chili powder (adjust to preference)
- 1 tbsp olive oil
- Salt to taste (use sparingly for DASH suitability)
- Fresh cilantro and lime wedges for serving (optional)

Directions:

1. Set the Instant Pot to 'Sauté' mode. Add olive oil, onions, and garlic, and sauté until translucent.
2. Add red bell pepper, cumin, smoked paprika, and chili powder. Stir well and cook for another 2 minutes.
3. Add the sweet potatoes, lentils, and vegetable broth to the pot. Secure the lid, set the valve to sealing, and select 'Manual' or 'Pressure Cook' for 20 minutes.
4. Allow for a natural pressure release after the cooking time ends. Once the pressure is fully released, open the lid, season with a small pinch of salt if needed, and give it a good stir.
5. Serve hot, garnished with fresh cilantro and a squeeze of lime if desired.

Nutritional Information: 280 calories, 15g protein, 49g carbohydrates, 3g fat, 12g fiber, 0mg cholesterol, 320mg sodium, 680mg potassium.

Seafood Gumbo

Yield: 4 servings | Prep time: 20 minutes | Cook time: 30 minutes

Ingredients:

- 1/2 lb shrimp, peeled and deveined
- 1/2 lb lump crab meat
- 1/4 lb cod or any white fish, diced
- 1 onion, diced
- 2 celery stalks, chopped
- 1 bell pepper, diced
- 3 cloves garlic, minced
- 1 can (14.5 oz) no-salt-added diced tomatoes
- 4 cups low-sodium vegetable or seafood broth
- 2 tsp olive oil
- 1/2 tsp smoked paprika
- 1/2 tsp ground black pepper
- 2 bay leaves
- 2 green onions, sliced (for garnish)
- Salt to taste (use sparingly for DASH suitability)
- Fresh parsley and lemon wedges for serving (optional)

Directions:

1. Set the Instant Pot to 'Sauté' mode. Add olive oil, onions, celery, bell pepper, and garlic. Sauté until vegetables are soft, about 5 minutes.
2. Add the smoked paprika, black pepper, and bay leaves. Stir for 1 minute until aromatic.
3. Pour in the diced tomatoes and broth, then add the seafood. Secure the lid, set the valve to sealing, and select 'Manual' or 'Pressure Cook' for 5 minutes.
4. Once the cooking time ends, do a quick pressure release. Remove bay leaves, season with a small pinch of salt if needed, and stir gently.
5. Serve the gumbo hot, garnished with green onions, fresh parsley, and a squeeze of lemon if desired.

Nutritional Information: 240 calories, 30g protein, 15g carbohydrates, 6g fat, 3g fiber, 180mg cholesterol, 380mg sodium, 650mg potassium.

Tomato Basil Bisque

Yield: 4 servings | Prep time: 10 minutes | Cook time: 20 minutes

Ingredients:

- 2 tbsp olive oil
- 1 onion, diced
- 3 cloves garlic, minced
- 1 can (28 oz) no-salt-added whole tomatoes
- 2 cups low-sodium vegetable broth
- 1 cup fresh basil leaves, chopped, plus more for garnish
- 1/2 cup unsweetened almond milk (or any other non-dairy milk)
- 1/2 tsp ground black pepper
- Salt to taste (use sparingly for DASH suitability)
- Fresh basil and shredded parmesan (optional, for garnish)

Directions:

1. Set the Instant Pot to 'Sauté' mode. Add olive oil, onions, and garlic. Sauté until the onions are translucent, about 3-4 minutes.
2. Add the whole tomatoes, breaking them up with a spoon. Add vegetable broth and chopped basil.
3. Secure the lid, set the valve to sealing, and select 'Manual' or 'Pressure Cook' for 10 minutes.
4. Once the cooking time ends, perform a quick pressure release. Use an immersion blender to puree the soup until smooth, then stir in the almond milk, ground black pepper, and a tiny pinch of salt if needed.
5. Serve hot, garnished with additional fresh basil and a sprinkle of shredded parmesan if desired.

Nutritional Information: 140 calories, 3g protein, 19g carbohydrates, 7g fat, 4g fiber, 0mg cholesterol, 150mg sodium, 450mg potassium.

Curried Carrot Soup

Yield: 4 servings | Prep time: 10 minutes | Cook time: 15 minutes

Ingredients:

- 2 tbsp olive oil
- 1 onion, diced
- 3 cloves garlic, minced
- 6 large carrots, peeled and chopped
- 4 cups low-sodium vegetable broth
- 1 tbsp curry powder (adjust to preference)
- 1 tsp ground ginger
- 1 cup unsweetened coconut milk
- Salt to taste (use sparingly for DASH suitability)
- Fresh cilantro leaves, for garnish

Directions:

1. Set the Instant Pot to 'Sauté' mode. Add olive oil, onions, and garlic. Sauté until onions are translucent, about 3 minutes.
2. Add chopped carrots, curry powder, ground ginger, and vegetable broth.
3. Secure the lid, set the valve to sealing, and select 'Manual' or 'Pressure Cook' for 10 minutes.
4. Once the cooking time ends, perform a quick pressure release. Use an immersion blender to puree the soup until smooth, then stir in the coconut milk. Season with a tiny pinch of salt if needed.
5. Serve hot, garnished with fresh cilantro leaves.

Nutritional Information: 165 calories, 3g protein, 21g carbohydrates, 9g fat, 5g fiber, 0mg cholesterol, 130mg sodium, 500mg potassium.

Rustic Potato Leek Soup

Yield: 4 servings | Prep time: 15 minutes | Cook time: 20 minutes

Ingredients:

- 2 tbsp olive oil
- 2 large leeks, white and light green parts only, cleaned and sliced
- 3 cloves garlic, minced
- 4 large russet potatoes, peeled and diced
- 4 cups low-sodium vegetable broth
- 1 bay leaf
- 1 tsp fresh thyme (or 1/2 tsp dried thyme)
- Salt to taste (use sparingly for DASH suitability)
- 1 cup unsweetened almond milk (or another low-fat milk alternative)
- Fresh parsley or chives, for garnish

Directions:

1. Set the Instant Pot to 'Sauté' mode. Add olive oil, leeks, and garlic. Sauté until leeks are softened, about 4 minutes.
2. Add diced potatoes, bay leaf, thyme, and vegetable broth.
3. Secure the lid, set the valve to sealing, and select 'Manual' or 'Pressure Cook' for 15 minutes.
4. Once the cooking time ends, perform a quick pressure release. Remove the bay leaf. Use an immersion blender to partially puree the soup, leaving some chunks for texture. Stir in the almond milk and season with a tiny pinch of salt if needed.
5. Serve hot, garnished with fresh parsley or chives.

Nutritional Information:200 calories, 4g protein, 38g carbohydrates, 5g fat, 5g fiber, 0mg cholesterol, 120mg sodium, 750mg potassium.

Vegetarian & Vegan Pleasures

Stuffed Bell Peppers with Quinoa

Yield: 4 servings | Prep time: 20 minutes | Cook time: 25 minutes

Ingredients:

- 4 large bell peppers, tops cut off and seeds removed
- 1 cup quinoa, rinsed and drained
- 2 cups low-sodium vegetable broth
- 1 tbsp olive oil
- 1 onion, finely chopped
- 2 garlic cloves, minced
- 1 zucchini, diced
- 1 can (14.5 oz) low-sodium diced tomatoes
- 1 tsp ground cumin
- 1 tsp paprika
- 1/2 tsp black pepper
- Salt to taste (use sparingly for DASH suitability)
- 1/4 cup fresh parsley or cilantro, chopped
- 1/2 cup low-fat feta cheese, crumbled (optional)

Directions:

1. On the 'Sauté' mode of the Instant Pot, heat olive oil and sauté onion, garlic, and zucchini until soft, about 4 minutes. Stir in quinoa, cumin, paprika, and pepper.
2. Add the diced tomatoes (with their juice) and vegetable broth to the pot. Mix well.
3. Stuff each bell pepper with the quinoa mixture and place them standing upright in the Instant Pot.
4. Secure the lid, set the valve to sealing, and select 'Manual' or 'Pressure Cook' for 15 minutes. Once done, allow a natural pressure release for 10 minutes followed by a quick release.
5. Carefully remove the peppers, top with parsley or cilantro, and optional feta cheese before serving.

Nutritional Information: 290 calories, 10g protein, 48g carbohydrates, 7g fat, 8g fiber, 5mg cholesterol, 170mg sodium, 800mg potassium.

Vegan Thai Green Curry

Yield: 4 servings | Prep time: 15 minutes | Cook time: 20 minutes

Ingredients:

- 1 tbsp olive oil or coconut oil
- 3 tbsp green curry paste (low-sodium or homemade)
- 1 can (14 oz) light coconut milk
- 2 cups low-sodium vegetable broth
- 1 cup cubed tofu, pressed and drained
- 1 zucchini, sliced
- 1 red bell pepper, sliced
- 1 cup snap peas or green beans, trimmed
- 1 cup diced eggplant
- 2 tsp low-sodium soy sauce or tamari
- 1 tsp coconut sugar or brown sugar
- 2 tbsp fresh lime juice
- 1/4 cup fresh basil, chopped
- Salt to taste (use sparingly for DASH suitability)

Directions:

1. Turn the Instant Pot to the 'Sauté' mode. Add oil and green curry paste, stirring until fragrant, about 2 minutes.
2. Stir in coconut milk and vegetable broth. Mix until the curry paste is well incorporated into the liquids.
3. Add tofu, zucchini, red bell pepper, snap peas, and eggplant to the pot. Stir to ensure everything is well coated with the curry mixture.
4. Secure the lid, set the valve to sealing, and select 'Manual' or 'Pressure Cook' for 8 minutes. After cooking, allow a quick release.
5. Stir in soy sauce, sugar, and lime juice. Taste and adjust seasonings if needed. Before serving, stir in fresh basil.

Nutritional Information: 230 calories, 9g protein, 20g carbohydrates, 14g fat, 4g fiber, 0mg cholesterol, 260mg sodium, 540mg potassium.

Spinach & Mushroom Lasagna

Yield: 4 servings | Prep time: 20 minutes | Cook time: 25 minutes

Ingredients:

- 8 whole wheat lasagna noodles
- 1 tbsp olive oil
- 2 cups fresh mushrooms, sliced
- 2 garlic cloves, minced
- 2 cups fresh spinach, chopped
- 2 cups low-sodium marinara sauce
- 1 1/2 cups ricotta cheese (part-skim)
- 1 cup mozzarella cheese (part-skim), shredded
- 1/4 cup grated Parmesan cheese
- 1/4 cup fresh basil, chopped
- 1/4 tsp black pepper
- 1/4 tsp dried oregano
- 1 cup water
- Salt to taste (use sparingly for DASH suitability)

Directions:

1. On the 'Sauté' mode of the Instant Pot, add olive oil, garlic, and mushrooms. Sauté until mushrooms are tender, about 4 minutes. Add spinach and stir until wilted. Turn off the sauté mode.
2. In a mixing bowl, combine ricotta cheese, half of the mozzarella, Parmesan, basil, oregano, and black pepper. Mix well.
3. Spread a layer of marinara sauce at the bottom of the pot. Place two lasagna noodles side by side, followed by a portion of the cheese mixture and then the spinach-mushroom mix. Repeat layers until all ingredients are used.
4. Pour water around the edges of the lasagna layers. Secure the Instant Pot lid and set to 'Manual' or 'Pressure Cook' for 8 minutes. Once done, allow a 10-minute natural release followed by a quick release.
5. Open the lid, sprinkle the remaining mozzarella on top, and let it melt with the residual heat. Allow the lasagna to sit for about 5 minutes before serving.

Nutritional Information: 450 calories, 25g protein, 40g carbohydrates, 20g fat, 6g fiber, 50mg cholesterol, 340mg sodium, 700mg potassium.

Moroccan Vegetable Tagine

Yield: 4 servings | Prep time: 15 minutes | Cook time: 20 minutes

Ingredients:

- 2 tbsp olive oil
- 1 large onion, finely chopped
- 3 garlic cloves, minced
- 1 tbsp ginger, freshly grated
- 1 tsp ground cumin
- 1 tsp ground coriander
- 1/2 tsp ground turmeric
- 1/4 tsp ground cinnamon
- 1/4 tsp cayenne pepper (adjust based on preference)
- 2 cups low-sodium vegetable broth
- 1 large sweet potato, cubed
- 2 carrots, sliced
- 1 zucchini, sliced
- 1 cup chickpeas, rinsed and drained
- 1 cup diced tomatoes (canned or fresh)
- 1/2 cup dried apricots, chopped
- Salt to taste (use sparingly for DASH suitability)
- Fresh cilantro and mint for garnish

Directions:

1. Turn the Instant Pot on 'Sauté' mode. Add olive oil, onion, garlic, and ginger, sautéing until the onion becomes translucent, about 3 minutes.
2. Add cumin, coriander, turmeric, cinnamon, and cayenne pepper, stirring well for another minute.
3. Incorporate sweet potato, carrots, zucchini, chickpeas, diced tomatoes, and dried apricots. Pour in the vegetable broth and mix thoroughly.
4. Secure the Instant Pot lid and set to 'Manual' or 'Pressure Cook' for 15 minutes. Once cooking completes, allow a 10-minute natural release followed by a quick release.
5. Open the lid, adjust seasoning if necessary, and serve garnished with fresh cilantro and mint.

Nutritional Information: 260 calories, 8g protein, 45g carbohydrates, 7g fat, 9g fiber, 0mg cholesterol, 220mg sodium, 750mg potassium.

Coconut Lime Tofu Curry

Yield: 4 servings | Prep time: 20 minutes | Cook time: 15 minutes

Ingredients:

- 14 oz firm tofu, cubed
- 1 tbsp olive oil
- 1 onion, finely chopped
- 3 garlic cloves, minced
- 1 tbsp ginger, freshly grated
- 1 tbsp curry powder
- 1/2 tsp turmeric powder
- 1 can (14 oz) light coconut milk
- Zest and juice of 1 lime
- 1 red bell pepper, sliced
- 1 zucchini, sliced
- 1 cup snap peas, trimmed
- Salt to taste (use sparingly for DASH suitability)
- Fresh cilantro for garnish
- 1 lime, sliced for serving

Directions:

1. Turn the Instant Pot on 'Sauté' mode. Add olive oil, onion, garlic, and ginger, sautéing until the onion is translucent, about 3 minutes.
2. Stir in the curry powder and turmeric, followed by the tofu cubes. Sauté for an additional 2 minutes to coat the tofu in spices.
3. Add the coconut milk, lime zest, lime juice, red bell pepper, zucchini, and snap peas to the pot. Stir everything together.
4. Secure the Instant Pot lid and set to 'Manual' or 'Pressure Cook' for 8 minutes. Once cooking completes, use a quick release. Adjust seasoning if necessary.
5. Serve hot, garnished with fresh cilantro and a slice of lime.

Nutritional Information: 320 calories, 14g protein, 25g carbohydrates, 20g fat, 6g fiber, 0mg cholesterol, 150mg sodium, 600mg potassium.

Eggplant Parmesan

Yield: 4 servings | Prep time: 15 minutes | Cook time: 20 minutes

Ingredients:

- 2 medium eggplants, sliced into 1/2-inch rounds
- 1 tbsp olive oil
- 1 small onion, finely chopped
- 2 garlic cloves, minced
- 1 can (14 oz) no-salt-added diced tomatoes
- 1/2 tsp dried basil
- 1/2 tsp dried oregano
- Salt to taste (use sparingly for DASH suitability)
- Freshly ground black pepper, to taste
- 1 cup low-fat mozzarella cheese, shredded
- 1/4 cup parmesan cheese, grated
- Fresh basil leaves, for garnish

Directions:

1. Turn the Instant Pot on 'Sauté' mode. Add olive oil, onion, and garlic, sautéing until the onion becomes translucent, about 3 minutes.
2. Add the diced tomatoes, dried basil, dried oregano, salt (if using), and black pepper. Stir and let it simmer for 2 minutes.
3. Layer the sliced eggplants in the Instant Pot over the sauce, ensuring even coverage. Sprinkle mozzarella and parmesan over the eggplant layers.
4. Secure the Instant Pot lid, set to 'Manual' or 'Pressure Cook' for 7 minutes. Once cooking is done, use a quick release.
5. Carefully open the lid. Serve the Eggplant Parmesan hot, garnished with fresh basil leaves.

Nutritional Information: 230 calories, 12g protein, 30g carbohydrates, 8g fat, 10g fiber, 20mg cholesterol, 280mg sodium, 700mg potassium.

Spaghetti Squash & Chickpea Ragout

Yield: 4 servings | Prep time: 10 minutes | Cook time: 25 minutes

Ingredients:

- 1 medium spaghetti squash, halved and seeds removed
- 1 can (14 oz) chickpeas, drained and rinsed
- 2 tbsp olive oil
- 1 small onion, diced
- 2 garlic cloves, minced
- 1 can (14 oz) no-salt-added diced tomatoes
- 1 tsp dried basil
- 1 tsp dried oregano
- Salt to taste (use sparingly for DASH suitability)
- Freshly ground black pepper, to taste
- 1/4 cup fresh parsley, chopped

Directions:

1. Pour 1 cup of water into the Instant Pot. Place the spaghetti squash halves (cut side up) on the steamer rack inside the pot. Secure the lid and set the pot to 'Manual' or 'Pressure Cook' for 7 minutes. Once done, use a quick release.
2. Remove the squash and set it aside. Empty the Instant Pot and switch it to 'Sauté' mode. Add olive oil, onion, and garlic, sautéing until the onion becomes translucent.
3. Add chickpeas, diced tomatoes, dried basil, dried oregano, salt (if using), and black pepper. Stir and let simmer for 3-5 minutes.
4. Using a fork, shred the spaghetti squash into strands and add it to the ragout. Stir well, let it simmer for another 2 minutes.
5. Serve hot, garnished with fresh parsley.

Nutritional Information: 275 calories, 9g protein, 45g carbohydrates, 9g fat, 10g fiber, 0mg cholesterol, 240mg sodium, 750mg potassium.

Vegan Jackfruit "Pulled Pork" Tacos

Yield: 4 servings | Prep time: 15 minutes | Cook time: 20 minutes

Ingredients:

- 2 cans (14 oz each) young green jackfruit in water, drained and rinsed
- 1 small onion, finely chopped
- 3 cloves garlic, minced
- 1 cup no-salt-added vegetable broth
- 2 tsp smoked paprika
- 1 tsp ground cumin
- 1/2 tsp black pepper
- 1/4 tsp chili powder (adjust for desired heat)
- 1 tbsp apple cider vinegar
- 1 tbsp olive oil
- 8 small whole wheat tortillas
- Toppings: shredded lettuce, diced tomatoes, sliced jalapeños, and lime wedges

Directions:

1. Using your fingers, shred the jackfruit into smaller pieces resembling pulled pork.
2. Turn on the Instant Pot to 'Sauté' mode. Add olive oil, followed by onion and garlic, sautéing until translucent.
3. Add the shredded jackfruit, smoked paprika, ground cumin, black pepper, chili powder, apple cider vinegar, and vegetable broth to the pot. Stir well.
4. Close the Instant Pot lid, set to 'Manual' or 'Pressure Cook' for 15 minutes. Once done, use a quick release.
5. Open the lid and stir. If the mixture is too watery, use the 'Sauté' mode to reduce and thicken the mixture for about 5 minutes. Adjust seasoning as needed.
6. Serve the jackfruit filling on whole wheat tortillas, topped with lettuce, tomatoes, jalapeños, and a squeeze of lime.

Nutritional Information: 310 calories, 6g protein, 62g carbohydrates, 5g fat, 9g fiber, 0mg cholesterol, 250mg sodium, 600mg potassium.

Ratatouille with Creamy Polenta

Yield: 4 servings | Prep time: 20 minutes | Cook time: 30 minutes

Ingredients:

For the Ratatouille:
- 1 medium zucchini, sliced into rounds
- 1 medium yellow squash, sliced into rounds
- 1 small eggplant, diced
- 1 red bell pepper, chopped
- 1 medium onion, chopped
- 3 cloves garlic, minced
- 1 can (14 oz) no-salt-added diced tomatoes
- 2 tbsp olive oil
- 1 tsp dried basil
- 1 tsp dried oregano
- 1/2 tsp black pepper

For the Creamy Polenta:
- 1 cup coarse-ground cornmeal (polenta)
- 4 cups low-sodium vegetable broth
- 1/4 cup nutritional yeast (or grated parmesan for non-vegan)
- 1 tbsp olive oil
- Pinch of salt

Directions:

1. Start by making the ratatouille. Turn on the Instant Pot to 'Sauté' mode. Add olive oil, followed by onion and garlic, sautéing until translucent. Add zucchini, yellow squash, eggplant, and bell pepper, sautéing for 5 minutes.
2. Add the canned tomatoes, basil, oregano, and black pepper. Mix well, then close the Instant Pot lid and set to 'Manual' or 'Pressure Cook' for 10 minutes. Once done, use a quick release.
3. For the polenta, remove the ratatouille from the Instant Pot and set aside. Combine vegetable broth, polenta, olive oil, and salt in the pot. Close the lid, set to 'Manual' or 'Pressure Cook' for 10 minutes. Quick release once done.
4. Stir in the nutritional yeast (or parmesan) until the polenta is creamy.
5. Serve the ratatouille over the creamy polenta, garnishing with fresh basil or parsley if desired.

Nutritional Information: 460 calories, 12g protein, 72g carbohydrates, 15g fat, 12g fiber, 0mg cholesterol, 280mg sodium, 1100mg potassium.

Butternut & Black Bean Chili

Yield: 4 servings | Prep time: 15 minutes | Cook time: 25 minutes

Ingredients:

- 2 cups butternut squash, peeled and cubed
- 1 can (15 oz) no-salt-added black beans, drained and rinsed
- 1 medium onion, chopped
- 2 cloves garlic, minced
- 1 can (14 oz) no-salt-added diced tomatoes
- 2 cups low-sodium vegetable broth

- 1 tsp ground cumin
- 1 tsp chili powder
- 1/2 tsp paprika
- 1/4 tsp black pepper
- 1 tbsp olive oil
- Fresh cilantro, for garnish (optional)
- 1 lime, cut into wedges (optional)

Directions:

1. Turn on the Instant Pot to 'Sauté' mode. Add olive oil, followed by the onions and garlic. Sauté until the onions become translucent.
2. Add the butternut squash cubes and sauté for another 2-3 minutes.
3. Add black beans, diced tomatoes, vegetable broth, cumin, chili powder, paprika, and black pepper. Stir to combine.
4. Close the Instant Pot lid and set it to 'Manual' or 'Pressure Cook' for 20 minutes. Once done, use a quick release.
5. Serve hot in bowls, garnished with fresh cilantro and lime wedges if desired.

Nutritional Information: 290 calories, 10g protein, 57g carbohydrates, 4g fat, 13g fiber, 0mg cholesterol, 220mg sodium, 1000mg potassium.

Vegetable Paella

Yield: 4 servings | Prep time: 20 minutes | Cook time: 30 minutes

Ingredients:

- 1 cup Arborio rice, rinsed
- 2 1/2 cups low-sodium vegetable broth
- 1 onion, finely chopped
- 2 cloves garlic, minced
- 1 bell pepper (red or yellow), sliced
- 1 small zucchini, diced
- 1/2 cup green beans, cut into 1-inch pieces
- 1/2 cup frozen peas

- 1/2 cup cherry tomatoes, halved
- 1 tsp turmeric powder
- 1 tsp paprika
- 1/4 tsp saffron threads (optional, for color and flavor)
- 1 tbsp olive oil
- Fresh parsley, chopped (for garnish)
- 1 lemon, cut into wedges

Directions:

1. Turn on the Instant Pot to 'Sauté' mode. Add olive oil, then sauté onion, garlic, bell pepper, and zucchini for 4-5 minutes or until onions are translucent.
2. Add Arborio rice, stirring for another 2 minutes to toast the rice slightly.
3. Pour in the vegetable broth, and then add green beans, peas, cherry tomatoes, turmeric, paprika, and saffron. Stir to combine.
4. Secure the Instant Pot lid and set to 'Slow Cook' for 30 minutes.
5. Once done, gently fluff the rice with a fork. Serve garnished with fresh parsley and lemon wedges.

Nutritional Information: 320 calories, 8g protein, 62g carbohydrates, 4g fat, 5g fiber, 0mg cholesterol, 150mg sodium, 450mg potassium.

Vegan Stuffed Cabbage Rolls

Yield: 4 servings | Prep time: 20 minutes | Cook time: 25 minutes

Ingredients:

- 8 large cabbage leaves, blanched
- 1 cup cooked brown rice
- 1 can (15 oz) lentils, drained and rinsed
- 1 small onion, finely chopped
- 2 cloves garlic, minced
- 1 carrot, finely grated
- 1 tbsp olive oil

- 2 cups low-sodium tomato sauce
- 1 tsp dried basil
- 1 tsp dried oregano
- Salt and pepper, to taste
- 1 cup water
- Fresh parsley, chopped (for garnish)

Directions:

1. On 'Sauté' mode, heat olive oil in the Instant Pot. Add onions and garlic, cooking until translucent. Add the carrot, lentils, rice, half the tomato sauce, basil, oregano, salt, and pepper, and stir well.
2. Lay each cabbage leaf flat and place a generous amount of the lentil and rice mixture in the center. Fold in the sides and roll up tightly.
3. Pour the remaining tomato sauce and water into the Instant Pot. Place the cabbage rolls seam-side down into the sauce.
4. Secure the lid, set the Instant Pot to 'Pressure Cook' on high for 15 minutes. Allow natural release.
5. Serve the cabbage rolls hot, garnished with fresh parsley.

Nutritional Information: 280 calories, 12g protein, 55g carbohydrates, 4g fat, 12g fiber, 0mg cholesterol, 220mg sodium, 800mg potassium.

Mushroom Stroganoff with Whole Wheat Noodles

Yield: 4 servings | Prep time: 15 minutes | Cook time: 20 minutes

Ingredients:

- 8 oz whole wheat noodles
- 2 tbsp olive oil
- 1 medium onion, finely chopped
- 3 cloves garlic, minced
- 1 lb fresh mushrooms, sliced (combination of button and cremini)
- 2 cups low-sodium vegetable broth

- 1 cup plain Greek yogurt (or vegan alternative)
- 2 tbsp whole wheat flour
- 1 tbsp low-sodium soy sauce or tamari
- 2 tsp dried thyme
- 1 tsp dried rosemary
- Salt and pepper, to taste
- Fresh parsley, chopped (for garnish)

Directions:

1. Turn the Instant Pot to 'Sauté' mode. Add olive oil, onions, and garlic. Cook until onions are translucent. Add mushrooms and sauté for another 5 minutes.
2. Stir in the flour until the mushrooms are coated. Add the vegetable broth, soy sauce, thyme, and rosemary. Mix well.
3. Add the whole wheat noodles, ensuring they are submerged in the liquid. Seal the Instant Pot and set to 'Pressure Cook' on high for 5 minutes.
4. After cooking, quick release the pressure. Stir in the Greek yogurt (or vegan alternative) until the sauce is creamy. Season with salt and pepper to taste.
5. Serve hot, garnished with fresh parsley.

Nutritional Information: 365 calories, 16g protein, 60g carbohydrates, 7g fat, 8g fiber, 5mg cholesterol, 230mg sodium, 550mg potassium.

Lentil & Mushroom Loaf

Yield: 4 servings | Prep time: 20 minutes | Cook time: 35 minutes

Ingredients:

- 1 cup dry green lentils, rinsed and drained
- 2 cups water
- 1 tbsp olive oil
- 1 medium onion, chopped
- 3 cloves garlic, minced
- 1 lb fresh mushrooms, finely chopped
- 1 cup whole wheat breadcrumbs
- 2 tbsp tomato paste
- 2 tbsp low-sodium soy sauce or tamari
- 1 tsp dried thyme
- 1 tsp dried rosemary
- Salt and black pepper, to taste
- Fresh parsley, chopped (for garnish)

Directions:

1. In the Instant Pot, combine lentils and water. Seal and set to 'Pressure Cook' on high for 15 minutes. Once done, quick release and drain any excess water.
2. On 'Sauté' mode, add olive oil, onions, garlic, and mushrooms. Cook until the mushrooms release their moisture and the mixture is fairly dry, about 7-8 minutes.
3. Add cooked lentils back into the pot. Stir in breadcrumbs, tomato paste, soy sauce, thyme, rosemary, salt, and pepper. Mix until everything is well combined.
4. Transfer the mixture into a silicone loaf pan that fits inside your Instant Pot. Pour 1 cup of water into the Instant Pot, place the trivet inside, and set the loaf pan on top. Seal the Instant Pot and set to 'Pressure Cook' on high for 20 minutes. Once done, allow a natural release for 10 minutes then quick release any remaining pressure.
5. Carefully remove the loaf from the Instant Pot. Let it cool slightly before slicing. Serve garnished with fresh parsley.

Nutritional Information:300 calories, 18g protein, 48g carbohydrates, 5g fat, 12g fiber, 0mg cholesterol, 280mg sodium, 750mg potassium.

Sweet Potato & Kale Tacos with Avocado Crema

Yield: 4 servings | Prep time: 15 minutes | Cook time: 20 minutes

Ingredients:

- 2 large sweet potatoes, peeled and diced
- 1 tbsp olive oil
- 3 cups kale, stems removed and roughly chopped
- 1/2 tsp ground cumin
- Salt and black pepper, to taste
- 8 small whole grain or corn tortillas
- 1 ripe avocado, pitted
- 1/4 cup plain Greek yogurt (or plant-based yogurt for vegan option)
- 1 lime, juiced
- 2 cloves garlic, minced
- 1/4 cup fresh cilantro, chopped
- 1/4 cup water, for pressure cooking

Directions:

1. Pour water into the Instant Pot. Add diced sweet potatoes in a steamer basket inside the pot. Seal and set to 'Pressure Cook' on high for 5 minutes. Once done, quick release the pressure. Remove sweet potatoes and set aside.
2. Set Instant Pot to 'Sauté' mode. Add olive oil, kale, cumin, salt, and pepper. Sauté until kale is wilted, about 3-4 minutes. Turn off the Instant Pot and stir in the cooked sweet potatoes.
3. For the avocado crema: In a blender, combine avocado, Greek yogurt, lime juice, garlic, cilantro, and a pinch of salt. Blend until smooth.
4. Warm the tortillas according to package directions. Fill each tortilla with sweet potato and kale mixture, and drizzle with avocado crema.
5. Serve immediately, garnished with additional cilantro if desired.

Nutritional Information:400 calories, 12g protein, 58g carbohydrates, 14g fat, 10g fiber, 3mg cholesterol, 320mg sodium, 800mg potassium.

Poultry & Meat Masterpieces

Herb-Crusted Turkey Breast

Yield: 4 servings | Prep time: 10 minutes | Cook time: 35 minutes

Ingredients:

- 2 lbs boneless, skinless turkey breast
- 1 tbsp olive oil
- 2 cloves garlic, minced
- 1 tsp dried rosemary
- 1 tsp dried thyme
- 1 tsp dried oregano
- Salt and black pepper, to taste
- 1/2 cup low-sodium chicken broth or water
- Zest from 1 lemon

Directions:

1. In a bowl, combine minced garlic, rosemary, thyme, oregano, lemon zest, olive oil, salt, and black pepper to form a paste.
2. Rub the herb paste all over the turkey breast, ensuring it's well coated.
3. Pour the low-sodium chicken broth or water into the Instant Pot. Place the turkey breast inside on the trivet.
4. Seal the Instant Pot and set to 'Pressure Cook' on high for 25 minutes. Once done, let the pressure release naturally for 10 minutes, then quick release the remaining pressure.
5. Remove the turkey breast, slice, and serve.

Nutritional Information: 250 calories, 40g protein, 3g carbohydrates, 8g fat, 1g fiber, 80mg cholesterol, 230mg sodium, 450mg potassium.

Beef Ragu

Yield: 4 servings | Prep time: 15 minutes | Cook time: 80 minutes

Ingredients:

- 1.5 lbs lean beef chuck, cubed
- 1 tbsp olive oil
- 1 medium onion, diced
- 3 cloves garlic, minced
- 1 carrot, finely chopped
- 1 celery stalk, finely chopped
- 1 can (14 oz) no-salt-added diced tomatoes
- 1/2 cup low-sodium beef broth
- 1 bay leaf
- 1 tsp dried rosemary
- 1 tsp dried thyme
- Salt and pepper, to taste
- Fresh parsley, chopped (for garnish)

Directions:

1. Set Instant Pot to 'Sauté' mode. Add olive oil, followed by onion, garlic, carrot, and celery. Sauté until softened.
2. Add beef cubes and sear on all sides until browned.
3. Add diced tomatoes, beef broth, bay leaf, rosemary, thyme, salt, and pepper. Mix well.
4. Seal the Instant Pot and set to 'Pressure Cook' on high for 75 minutes. Once done, allow the pressure to release naturally.
5. Discard the bay leaf, stir well, and serve the ragu garnished with fresh parsley.

Nutritional Information: 370 calories, 40g protein, 20g carbohydrates, 15g fat, 4g fiber, 100mg cholesterol, 250mg sodium, 800mg potassium.

Rosemary Lemon Chicken Thighs

Yield: 4 servings | Prep time: 10 minutes | Cook time: 25 minutes

Ingredients:

- 4 boneless, skinless chicken thighs
- 1 tbsp olive oil
- 3 cloves garlic, minced
- 1 lemon, zested and juiced
- 2 tsp fresh rosemary, finely chopped
- 1 cup low-sodium chicken broth
- Salt and pepper, to taste
- 1 tbsp cornstarch mixed with 2 tbsp water (optional, for thickening)

Directions:

1. In a bowl, combine lemon zest, lemon juice, rosemary, garlic, salt, and pepper. Marinate the chicken thighs in this mixture for at least 10 minutes.
2. Set the Instant Pot to 'Sauté' mode and heat the olive oil. Add the chicken thighs and sear on both sides until golden brown.
3. Pour in the low-sodium chicken broth and deglaze the bottom of the pot.
4. Seal the Instant Pot and set to 'Pressure Cook' on high for 15 minutes. Once done, allow the pressure to release naturally.
5. If a thicker sauce is desired, set the pot to 'Sauté' mode again, add the cornstarch mixture, and stir until the sauce has thickened.

Nutritional Information: 250 calories, 28g protein, 5g carbohydrates, 12g fat, 1g fiber, 110mg cholesterol, 200mg sodium, 400mg potassium.

Spiced Pork Tenderloin with Apples

Yield: 4 servings | Prep time: 15 minutes | Cook time: 20 minutes

Ingredients:

- 1 pork tenderloin (about 1 lb.)
- 2 tbsp olive oil
- 2 medium apples, cored and sliced
- 1 onion, thinly sliced
- 2 cloves garlic, minced
- 1 tsp ground cinnamon
- 1/2 tsp ground nutmeg
- 1/4 tsp ground cloves
- 1 cup low-sodium chicken broth
- Salt and pepper, to taste

Directions:

1. In a bowl, season the pork tenderloin with salt, pepper, cinnamon, nutmeg, and cloves. Let it marinate for at least 10 minutes.
2. Set the Instant Pot to 'Sauté' mode and heat the olive oil. Sear the pork tenderloin on all sides until browned.
3. Add the onions, garlic, and apples, and continue sautéing for another 2-3 minutes.
4. Pour in the low-sodium chicken broth. Seal the Instant Pot lid and set it to 'Pressure Cook' for 15 minutes. Once done, let the pressure release naturally.
5. Transfer the pork to a cutting board and slice. Serve with the apple-onion mixture from the pot.

Nutritional Information: 280 calories, 30g protein, 20g carbohydrates, 9g fat, 3g fiber, 80mg cholesterol, 150mg sodium, 550mg potassium.

Moroccan Chicken with Apricots

Yield: 4 servings | Prep time: 20 minutes | Cook time: 25 minutes

Ingredients:

- 4 boneless, skinless chicken breasts
- 1 cup dried apricots, halved
- 1 large onion, finely chopped
- 2 cloves garlic, minced
- 1 tsp ground cinnamon
- 1 tsp ground cumin
- 1/2 tsp ground turmeric

- 1/4 tsp ground ginger
- 1/4 tsp ground coriander
- 2 cups low-sodium chicken broth
- 1 tbsp olive oil
- Salt and pepper, to taste
- Fresh cilantro, for garnish

Directions:

1. Set the Instant Pot to 'Sauté' mode. Heat the olive oil and sauté the onions and garlic until translucent.
2. Season the chicken breasts with salt, pepper, and the other spices. Add to the pot and sear each side for about 2 minutes.
3. Add the dried apricots and pour in the low-sodium chicken broth. Ensure that the chicken is covered with the liquid.
4. Seal the Instant Pot lid and set it to 'Pressure Cook' for 20 minutes. Once done, let the pressure release naturally.
5. Serve the chicken with the apricots and sauce, garnished with fresh cilantro.

Nutritional Information: 320 calories, 35g protein, 25g carbohydrates, 8g fat, 3g fiber, 85mg cholesterol, 200mg sodium, 600mg potassium.

Beef and Broccoli Stir Fry

Yield: 4 servings | Prep time: 15 minutes | Cook time: 10 minutes

Ingredients:

- 1 lb lean beef steak (like sirloin), thinly sliced
- 2 cups broccoli florets
- 1 medium onion, thinly sliced
- 2 cloves garlic, minced
- 1/4 cup low-sodium soy sauce
- 1/4 cup beef broth or water

- 2 tbsp cornstarch
- 1 tbsp olive oil
- 1 tsp ground ginger
- 1 tsp sesame oil (optional for flavor)
- 1 tbsp sesame seeds (for garnish)
- Green onions, sliced (for garnish)

Directions:

1. Set the Instant Pot to 'Sauté' mode. Add olive oil and sauté beef slices until they are browned on all sides. Remove and set aside.
2. In the same pot, add onions and garlic, sautéing until translucent. Add ground ginger and stir well.
3. In a small bowl, whisk together the low-sodium soy sauce, beef broth, and cornstarch. Pour this mixture into the Instant Pot.
4. Add the beef back to the pot, followed by the broccoli florets. Close the lid and set the pot to 'Pressure Cook' for 3 minutes.
5. Quick-release the pressure. Stir in sesame oil if using. Serve hot, garnished with sesame seeds and green onions.

Nutritional Information: 300 calories, 32g protein, 18g carbohydrates, 10g fat, 3g fiber, 70mg cholesterol, 400mg sodium, 650mg potassium.

Chicken Alfredo with Whole Wheat Pasta

Yield: 4 servings | Prep time: 10 minutes | Cook time: 20 minutes

Ingredients:

- 2 chicken breasts, boneless and skinless, cut into bite-sized pieces
- 8 oz whole wheat fettuccine or linguine
- 2 cups low-sodium chicken broth
- 1 cup low-fat milk or unsweetened almond milk
- 2 cloves garlic, minced
- 1/2 cup grated Parmesan cheese
- 1/2 cup low-fat Greek yogurt or low-fat cream cheese
- 1 tbsp olive oil
- 1 tsp dried Italian herbs
- Salt and pepper to taste
- Fresh parsley, chopped (for garnish)
- Red pepper flakes (optional, for garnish)

Directions:

1. Set the Instant Pot to 'Sauté' mode. Add olive oil and sauté chicken pieces until lightly browned. Add garlic and sauté for another minute.
2. Add the whole wheat pasta, ensuring it is broken in half if needed to fit. Pour in the chicken broth and milk. Ensure the pasta is submerged in the liquid.
3. Lock the Instant Pot lid and set to 'Pressure Cook' on high for 8 minutes. Once done, quick release the pressure.
4. Stir in the Greek yogurt or cream cheese, Parmesan cheese, dried herbs, salt, and pepper. Mix until a creamy sauce forms. Let sit for a few minutes to thicken.
5. Serve hot, garnished with fresh parsley and optional red pepper flakes.

Nutritional Information:450 calories, 40g protein, 55g carbohydrates, 10g fat, 7g fiber, 85mg cholesterol, 320mg sodium, 650mg potassium.

Lamb with Garlic & Rosemary

Yield: 4 servings | Prep time: 15 minutes | Cook time: 60 minutes

Ingredients:

- 2 lbs lamb shoulder, trimmed of excess fat
- 4 cloves garlic, minced
- 2 tbsp fresh rosemary, finely chopped
- 1 cup low-sodium beef or vegetable broth
- 1 tbsp olive oil
- Salt and pepper to taste
- 1 tbsp cornstarch (optional, for thickening)
- Fresh lemon zest (for garnish)
- Additional fresh rosemary sprigs (for garnish)

Directions:

1. Rub the lamb with garlic, chopped rosemary, salt, and pepper. Let it marinate for at least 30 minutes for better flavor, if time permits.
2. Set the Instant Pot to 'Sauté' mode. Add olive oil and sear the lamb on all sides until browned.
3. Pour in the low-sodium broth. Ensure the bottom of the pot is deglazed by scraping up any brown bits with a wooden spoon.
4. Lock the Instant Pot lid and set to 'Pressure Cook' on high for 60 minutes. Once done, natural release for 15 minutes, then quick release any remaining pressure.
5. (Optional) For a thicker sauce, create a slurry by mixing cornstarch with 2 tbsp cold water. Set the Instant Pot to 'Sauté' mode again, and stir in the slurry. Cook until the sauce thickens.
6. Serve the lamb hot, garnished with fresh lemon zest and rosemary sprigs.

Nutritional Information:430 calories, 48g protein, 5g carbohydrates, 25g fat, 1g fiber, 140mg cholesterol, 300mg sodium, 650mg potassium.

Lemon Herb Roasted Chicken

Yield: 4 servings | Prep time: 20 minutes | Cook time: 25 minutes

Ingredients:

- 4 boneless, skinless chicken breasts
- Zest and juice of 1 lemon
- 2 tbsp fresh rosemary, finely chopped
- 2 tbsp fresh thyme, finely chopped
- 1 tbsp olive oil
- 1 cup low-sodium chicken broth
- 4 cloves garlic, minced
- Salt and pepper to taste
- Fresh lemon slices and additional herbs (for garnish)

Directions:

1. In a bowl, mix lemon zest, lemon juice, rosemary, thyme, garlic, olive oil, salt, and pepper. Rub this mixture all over the chicken breasts and let marinate for at least 15 minutes.
2. Set the Instant Pot to 'Sauté' mode. Add the chicken breasts and sear on both sides until lightly browned.
3. Add the low-sodium chicken broth, ensuring the bottom of the pot is deglazed by scraping up any brown bits with a wooden spoon.
4. Lock the Instant Pot lid and set to 'Pressure Cook' on high for 15 minutes. Once done, quick release the pressure.
5. Serve the chicken hot, garnished with fresh lemon slices and additional herbs.

Nutritional Information: 260 calories, 32g protein, 6g carbohydrates, 12g fat, 1g fiber, 85mg cholesterol, 220mg sodium, 550mg potassium.

Beef Stew with Root Vegetables

Yield: 4 servings | Prep time: 25 minutes | Cook time: 35 minutes

Ingredients:

- 1 lb lean beef stew meat, cut into 1-inch pieces
- 2 cups low-sodium beef broth
- 2 medium carrots, peeled and sliced
- 2 medium parsnips, peeled and sliced
- 1 medium turnip, peeled and diced
- 2 medium potatoes, peeled and diced
- 1 onion, chopped
- 2 cloves garlic, minced
- 2 tsp olive oil
- 1 tsp dried rosemary
- 1 tsp dried thyme
- Salt and pepper to taste
- 2 tbsp whole wheat flour
- Fresh parsley for garnish

Directions:

1. Turn the Instant Pot to 'Sauté' mode. Add olive oil, then add beef stew meat and brown on all sides. Sprinkle the beef with whole wheat flour, ensuring all pieces are coated.
2. Add onion and garlic to the pot, stirring until onions are translucent.
3. Pour in the low-sodium beef broth, scraping the bottom of the pot to lift any brown bits. Then add carrots, parsnips, turnip, potatoes, rosemary, thyme, salt, and pepper.
4. Lock the Instant Pot lid, set the valve to 'Sealing,' and cook on 'Pressure Cook' high for 30 minutes. Once done, allow a natural pressure release for 10 minutes before doing a quick release.
5. Serve hot, garnished with fresh parsley.

Nutritional Information: 325 calories, 28g protein, 40g carbohydrates, 7g fat, 7g fiber, 60mg cholesterol, 350mg sodium, 1000mg potassium.

Tarragon Chicken with Spring Vegetables

Yield: 4 servings | Prep time: 20 minutes | Cook time: 25 minutes

Ingredients:

- 4 boneless, skinless chicken breasts
- 1 cup low-sodium chicken broth
- 1 cup chopped asparagus
- 1 cup green peas (fresh or frozen)
- 1 cup diced zucchini
- 1 medium leek, cleaned and sliced
- 2 tbsp fresh tarragon, finely chopped
- 2 tbsp olive oil
- 2 cloves garlic, minced
- 1/2 cup non-fat plain Greek yogurt
- Salt and pepper to taste
- Zest of 1 lemon
- 1 tbsp lemon juice

Directions:

1. Turn the Instant Pot to 'Sauté' mode. Add olive oil, then chicken breasts. Brown both sides of the chicken, then remove and set aside.
2. Add leek and garlic to the pot, stirring until softened. Deglaze with a splash of the chicken broth, scraping the bottom of the pot.
3. Return the chicken to the pot. Pour over the remaining broth, asparagus, peas, zucchini, lemon zest, and lemon juice. Sprinkle with salt, pepper, and half of the tarragon.
4. Close the lid, set the valve to 'Sealing', and select 'Pressure Cook' on high for 15 minutes. When done, quick release the pressure.
5. Stir in Greek yogurt and remaining tarragon before serving.

Nutritional Information: 285 calories, 30g protein, 15g carbohydrates, 10g fat, 4g fiber, 85mg cholesterol, 250mg sodium, 600mg potassium.

Pulled Pork with Pineapple Slaw

Yield: 4 servings | Prep time: 20 minutes | Cook time: 90 minutes

Ingredients:

For the Pulled Pork:
- 2 lbs pork shoulder, trimmed of excess fat
- 1 cup low-sodium chicken broth
- 2 cloves garlic, minced
- 1 tbsp apple cider vinegar
- 1 tsp smoked paprika
- 1 tsp ground cumin
- Salt and pepper to taste

For the Pineapple Slaw:

- 2 cups shredded green cabbage
- 1 cup diced fresh pineapple
- 1/2 red bell pepper, thinly sliced
- 1/4 cup thinly sliced red onion
- 1/4 cup chopped fresh cilantro
- 2 tbsp low-fat Greek yogurt
- 1 tbsp apple cider vinegar
- Salt and pepper to taste

Directions:

1. Combine pork shoulder, chicken broth, garlic, apple cider vinegar, smoked paprika, cumin, salt, and pepper in the Instant Pot. Close the lid, set to 'Sealing', and select 'Pressure Cook' on high for 90 minutes. When done, allow natural release for 10 minutes, then quick release the remaining pressure.
2. While pork is cooking, prepare the slaw: In a large bowl, combine cabbage, pineapple, bell pepper, red onion, and cilantro. In a separate smaller bowl, whisk together Greek yogurt, apple cider vinegar, salt, and pepper. Pour the dressing over the slaw mixture and toss to combine.
3. Once the pork is done and the pressure is released, shred it using two forks directly in the pot, mixing with the juices.
4. Serve pulled pork on plates or whole wheat buns, topped with pineapple slaw.

Nutritional Information: 450 calories, 40g protein, 30g carbohydrates, 15g fat, 5g fiber, 120mg cholesterol, 350mg sodium, 700mg potassium.

Honey Mustard Glazed Chicken

Yield: 4 servings | Prep time: 10 minutes | Cook time: 15 minutes

Ingredients:

- 4 boneless, skinless chicken breasts (about 1.5 lbs)
- 1/4 cup low-sodium chicken broth
- 2 tbsp honey
- 2 tbsp Dijon mustard
- 1 tbsp apple cider vinegar
- 1 clove garlic, minced
- 1/2 tsp dried thyme
- Salt and pepper to taste
- 1 tbsp olive oil
- Chopped parsley for garnish (optional)

Directions:

1. In a small bowl, whisk together honey, Dijon mustard, apple cider vinegar, garlic, thyme, salt, and pepper. Set aside.
2. Turn the Instant Pot to 'Sauté' mode and heat olive oil. Once hot, add the chicken breasts and brown them for 2-3 minutes on each side.
3. Pour the chicken broth into the pot and deglaze by scraping the bottom of the pot to release any bits stuck to it.
4. Pour the prepared honey mustard mixture over the chicken breasts, ensuring they are coated well.
5. Secure the Instant Pot lid, set the valve to 'Sealing', and select 'Pressure Cook' or 'Manual' on high for 10 minutes. Once done, allow a natural pressure release for 5 minutes before performing a quick release.

Nutritional Information: 280 calories, 30g protein, 15g carbohydrates, 10g fat, 1g fiber, 85mg cholesterol, 220mg sodium, 320mg potassium.

Spicy Beef & Bean Chili

Yield: 4 servings | Prep time: 15 minutes | Cook time: 30 minutes

Ingredients:

- 1 lb lean ground beef
- 1 can (15 oz) low-sodium black beans, drained and rinsed
- 1 can (15 oz) low-sodium kidney beans, drained and rinsed
- 1 can (14.5 oz) low-sodium diced tomatoes
- 1 onion, diced
- 3 cloves garlic, minced
- 2 tbsp chili powder
- 1 tsp cumin
- 1/2 tsp cayenne pepper (adjust according to heat preference)
- 1 cup low-sodium beef broth
- 1 bell pepper, diced
- Salt and pepper to taste
- 1 tbsp olive oil
- Optional toppings: diced avocado, low-fat sour cream, chopped cilantro

Directions:

1. Turn the Instant Pot to 'Sauté' mode and heat olive oil. Add onions, bell pepper, and garlic, sautéing until soft.
2. Add the ground beef and cook until browned. Drain any excess fat.
3. Add the beans, tomatoes, chili powder, cumin, cayenne pepper, salt, pepper, and beef broth. Stir well to combine.
4. Secure the lid, set the valve to 'Sealing', and select 'Pressure Cook' or 'Manual' on high for 25 minutes. Once done, allow a natural pressure release for 10 minutes before performing a quick release.

Nutritional Information: 450 calories, 32g protein, 55g carbohydrates, 10g fat, 15g fiber, 70mg cholesterol, 420mg sodium, 980mg potassium.

Sustainably Sourced Seafood Dishes

Lemon Garlic Shrimp Scampi

Yield: 4 servings | Prep time: 10 minutes | Cook time: 5 minutes

Ingredients:

- 1 lb large shrimp, peeled and deveined
- 8 oz whole wheat spaghetti or linguine
- 3 cloves garlic, minced
- Zest and juice of 1 lemon
- 1/4 cup fresh parsley, chopped
- 1 tbsp olive oil
- 1/2 cup low-sodium chicken or vegetable broth
- 1/4 tsp crushed red pepper flakes (optional)
- Salt and pepper to taste
- 1/4 cup grated Parmesan cheese (optional for garnish)

Directions:

1. Turn on the Instant Pot's 'Sauté' mode. Add olive oil and garlic, sautéing until fragrant.
2. Add the broth, lemon zest, lemon juice, and spaghetti (broken in half). Ensure the spaghetti is submerged in the liquid.
3. Close the lid and set the Instant Pot to 'Manual' or 'Pressure Cook' on high for 4 minutes. Once done, perform a quick release.
4. Open the lid, add in the shrimp, parsley, red pepper flakes, salt, and pepper. Stir well, then close the lid and let it sit for 5 minutes to allow the shrimp to cook in the residual heat.
5. Garnish with Parmesan cheese before serving if desired.

Nutritional Information:320 calories, 28g protein, 45g carbohydrates, 5g fat, 6g fiber, 165mg cholesterol, 320mg sodium, 250mg potassium.

Salmon with Dill & Lemon

Yield: 4 servings | Prep time: 5 minutes | Cook time: 15 minutes

Ingredients:

- 4 salmon fillets (about 6 oz each)
- 1 cup water
- 2 lemons: zest of one, and both thinly sliced
- 2 tbsp fresh dill, chopped
- 1 garlic clove, minced
- 1 tbsp olive oil
- Salt and pepper to taste

Directions:

1. In the Instant Pot, add water, then place the trivet or a steamer basket inside.
2. Lay the salmon fillets on the trivet or basket. Drizzle with olive oil, sprinkle with garlic, lemon zest, and season with salt and pepper. Place lemon slices on top of the salmon fillets.
3. Close the Instant Pot lid, set the vent to 'Sealing', and set it to 'Steam' mode for 3 minutes.
4. Once the cooking cycle completes, allow the pressure to naturally release for 5 minutes, then perform a quick release. Sprinkle the fresh dill over the salmon before serving.

Nutritional Information:250 calories, 34g protein, 3g carbohydrates, 11g fat, 1g fiber, 75mg cholesterol, 75mg sodium, 650mg potassium.

Seafood Paella with Saffron Rice

Yield: 4 servings | Prep time: 20 minutes | Cook time: 25 minutes

Ingredients:

- 1 cup long-grain brown rice
- 2 cups low-sodium chicken or vegetable broth
- 1/4 tsp saffron threads
- 8 oz shrimp, peeled and deveined
- 8 oz mussels, cleaned
- 8 oz clams, cleaned
- 1/2 cup diced tomatoes (canned, no salt added)
- 1 bell pepper, thinly sliced
-

- 1 small onion, finely chopped
- 2 cloves garlic, minced
- 2 tbsp olive oil
- 1 tsp smoked paprika
- 1/4 cup fresh parsley, chopped
- 1 lemon, cut into wedges for garnish
- Salt and pepper to taste

Directions:

1. In a bowl, soak the saffron threads in 2 tablespoons of warm broth. Set aside.
2. Turn on the Instant Pot's 'Sauté' mode. Add olive oil, onions, and garlic, and cook until onions are translucent.
3. Stir in the rice, smoked paprika, tomatoes, and bell pepper. Add the saffron-infused broth and the remaining broth. Mix well.
4. Arrange the shrimp, mussels, and clams on top of the rice mixture. Close the Instant Pot lid, set the vent to 'Sealing', and set it to 'Pressure Cook' or 'Manual' mode for 10 minutes.
5. Once the cooking cycle completes, allow the pressure to naturally release for 10 minutes, then perform a quick release. Discard any mussels or clams that did not open. Garnish with parsley and lemon wedges before serving.

Nutritional Information:350 calories, 28g protein, 45g carbohydrates, 7g fat, 4g fiber, 85mg cholesterol, 220mg sodium, 650mg potassium.

Clam & Corn Chowder

Yield: 4 servings | Prep time: 15 minutes | Cook time: 20 minutes

Ingredients:

- 2 cans (6.5 oz each) chopped clams in juice, undrained
- 3 cups fresh or frozen corn kernels
- 2 cups low-sodium vegetable broth
- 1 cup diced potatoes, skin on
- 1/2 cup diced celery
- 1/2 cup diced carrots

- 1 small onion, chopped
- 2 cloves garlic, minced
- 1 cup low-fat milk or unsweetened almond milk
- 2 tbsp olive oil
- 1/4 tsp dried thyme
- Salt and pepper to taste
- Fresh chives, chopped, for garnish

Directions:

1. Turn on the Instant Pot's 'Sauté' mode. Add olive oil, onions, celery, carrots, and garlic. Cook until onions become translucent.
2. Add potatoes, corn, chopped clams with their juice, thyme, and low-sodium vegetable broth to the pot. Stir well.
3. Close the Instant Pot lid, set the vent to 'Sealing', and set it to 'Pressure Cook' or 'Manual' mode for 10 minutes.
4. Once the cooking cycle is done, allow the pressure to naturally release for 5 minutes, then perform a quick release. Stir in the milk and let the chowder sit for 5 minutes to heat through.
5. Serve hot, garnished with fresh chives.

Nutritional Information:280 calories, 18g protein, 40g carbohydrates, 6g fat, 5g fiber, 45mg cholesterol, 320mg sodium, 700mg potassium.

Mussels in Tomato Wine Broth

Yield: 4 servings | Prep time: 10 minutes | Cook time: 8 minutes

Ingredients:

- 2 lbs fresh mussels, cleaned and debearded
- 1 can (14 oz) low-sodium diced tomatoes, undrained
- 1 cup dry white wine (like Chardonnay)
- 1/2 cup chopped fresh parsley
- 4 cloves garlic, minced
- 1 small onion, finely chopped
- 2 tbsp olive oil
- 1/4 tsp red pepper flakes (adjust to taste)
- Salt and pepper to taste
- 1 lemon, zested and juiced

Directions:

1. Turn on the Instant Pot's 'Sauté' mode. Add olive oil, onions, and garlic. Cook until onions become translucent.
2. Add the white wine, allowing it to simmer for 2 minutes, then add the diced tomatoes, red pepper flakes, half of the parsley, lemon zest, and lemon juice. Stir well.
3. Add the cleaned mussels to the pot and give them a quick stir.
4. Close the Instant Pot lid, set the vent to 'Sealing', and set it to 'Manual' or 'Pressure Cook' mode for 4 minutes.
5. Once the cooking cycle is complete, perform a quick release. Discard any mussels that have not opened. Sprinkle with the remaining fresh parsley before serving.

Nutritional Information: 220 calories, 24g protein, 15g carbohydrates, 7g fat, 2g fiber, 50mg cholesterol, 330mg sodium, 500mg potassium.

Cajun Catfish Stew

Yield: 4 servings | Prep time: 15 minutes | Cook time: 20 minutes

Ingredients:

- 1 lb catfish fillets, cut into 2-inch pieces
- 1 can (14 oz) low-sodium diced tomatoes, undrained
- 1 bell pepper, chopped
- 1 onion, chopped
- 3 garlic cloves, minced
- 2 celery stalks, chopped
- 1 cup low-sodium chicken or vegetable broth
- 2 tsp olive oil
- 1 tsp Cajun seasoning (low-sodium preferred)
- 1/2 tsp paprika
- 1/2 tsp black pepper
- 2 bay leaves
- 1/4 cup chopped fresh parsley
- 1 lemon, zested and juiced

Directions:

1. Turn on the Instant Pot's 'Sauté' mode. Add olive oil, onions, bell pepper, celery, and garlic. Sauté until vegetables are tender.
2. Stir in the diced tomatoes, chicken or vegetable broth, Cajun seasoning, paprika, black pepper, and bay leaves.
3. Place the catfish pieces on top, making sure they are submerged in the liquid.
4. Close the Instant Pot lid, set the vent to 'Sealing', and set it to 'Manual' or 'Pressure Cook' mode for 8 minutes.
5. Once the cooking cycle is complete, perform a quick release. Remove the bay leaves, stir in lemon zest, lemon juice, and fresh parsley before serving.

Nutritional Information: 210 calories, 23g protein, 12g carbohydrates, 7g fat, 3g fiber, 55mg cholesterol, 320mg sodium, 400mg potassium.

Seafood & Sausage Gumbo

Yield: 4 servings | Prep time: 20 minutes | Cook time: 30 minutes

Ingredients:

- 1/2 lb shrimp, peeled and deveined
- 1/2 lb andouille sausage, sliced (low-sodium variety)
- 1/2 lb lump crab meat
- 1 cup okra, chopped
- 1 onion, chopped
- 1 bell pepper, chopped
- 3 garlic cloves, minced
- 2 cups low-sodium chicken broth
- 1 can (14 oz) low-sodium diced tomatoes, undrained
- 2 tsp olive oil
- 2 tsp Cajun seasoning (low-sodium preferred)
- 1 bay leaf
- 1/4 cup fresh parsley, chopped
- 2 green onions, chopped
- 1/4 tsp black pepper

Directions:

1. Using the 'Sauté' mode on the Instant Pot, add olive oil, onions, bell pepper, garlic, and sausage slices. Cook until the vegetables are soft and the sausage is slightly browned.
2. Add the diced tomatoes, chicken broth, Cajun seasoning, okra, bay leaf, and black pepper. Stir well.
3. Place the lid on the Instant Pot, set the vent to 'Sealing', and set it to 'Manual' or 'Pressure Cook' mode for 20 minutes.
4. Perform a quick release. Add the shrimp and crab meat, stirring them into the mixture. Place the lid back on for 5 minutes, allowing the residual heat to cook the seafood.
5. Before serving, discard the bay leaf and sprinkle with fresh parsley and green onions.

Nutritional Information:280 calories, 25g protein, 15g carbohydrates, 12g fat, 3g fiber, 115mg cholesterol, 380mg sodium, 550mg potassium.

Poached Salmon with Caper Sauce

Yield: 4 servings | Prep time: 15 minutes | Cook time: 10 minutes

Ingredients:

- 4 salmon fillets (about 6 oz each)
- 2 cups low-sodium vegetable broth
- 1/4 cup capers, rinsed and drained
- 1/2 cup plain Greek yogurt (low-fat)
- 1 tbsp fresh lemon juice
- 2 garlic cloves, minced
- 2 tbsp fresh dill, chopped
- 1 tsp olive oil
- 1/2 tsp black pepper
- 1/4 tsp salt (optional)

Directions:

1. Place the salmon fillets in the Instant Pot and add the vegetable broth. Ensure salmon is submerged, if not, add enough water just to cover.
2. Close the lid, set the vent to 'Sealing', and select 'Manual' or 'Pressure Cook' for 5 minutes.
3. While the salmon is cooking, in a small bowl, mix together the Greek yogurt, capers, lemon juice, garlic, dill, olive oil, black pepper, and salt if desired. Set aside.
4. Once the cooking cycle completes, perform a quick release. Carefully remove the salmon fillets from the Instant Pot and plate.
5. Drizzle the prepared caper sauce over the salmon before serving.

Nutritional Information:280 calories, 34g protein, 5g carbohydrates, 12g fat, 1g fiber, 75mg cholesterol, 380mg sodium, 800mg potassium.

Thai Coconut Fish Curry

Yield: 4 servings | Prep time: 20 minutes | Cook time: 15 minutes

Ingredients:

- 1 lb white fish fillets (like cod or halibut), cut into chunks
- 1 can (14 oz) light coconut milk
- 2 tbsp Thai red curry paste
- 1 tbsp low-sodium soy sauce
- 2 tsp fresh ginger, grated
- 2 garlic cloves, minced
- 1 bell pepper, sliced
- 1/2 cup snap peas
- 1 tbsp lime juice
- 2 tbsp fresh cilantro, chopped
- 1 tbsp olive oil
- 1/4 tsp salt (optional)
- 1/2 tsp black pepper

Directions:

1. Turn on the Instant Pot to 'Sauté' mode and heat the olive oil. Add ginger and garlic, stirring for about 1 minute.
2. Add Thai red curry paste and stir until fragrant, about 2 minutes. Pour in the coconut milk and stir until smooth.
3. Add fish chunks, bell pepper, snap peas, low-sodium soy sauce, salt (if using), and black pepper. Gently mix to combine.
4. Secure the lid, set the vent to 'Sealing', and select 'Manual' or 'Pressure Cook' for 5 minutes.
5. Once done, perform a quick release. Stir in lime juice and garnish with fresh cilantro before serving.

Nutritional Information: 260 calories, 27g protein, 9g carbohydrates, 14g fat, 2g fiber, 60mg cholesterol, 270mg sodium, 550mg potassium.

Rustic Seafood Stew

Honey Lime Glazed Tilapia

Yield: 4 servings | Prep time: 10 minutes | Cook time: 10 minutes

Ingredients:

- 4 tilapia fillets (about 4 oz each)
- 3 tbsp honey
- Zest and juice of 2 limes
- 2 garlic cloves, minced
- 1/2 tsp black pepper
- 1/4 tsp salt (optional for DASH)
- 1 tbsp olive oil
- 1/4 cup water
- Fresh cilantro or parsley for garnish (optional)

Directions:

1. In a bowl, whisk together honey, lime zest, lime juice, garlic, black pepper, and salt (if using) to create the glaze.
2. Turn the Instant Pot on 'Sauté' mode. Once hot, add olive oil and sear tilapia fillets on both sides for about 1 minute each. Remove and set aside.
3. Add water to the pot, followed by the trivet. Place the tilapia fillets on the trivet.
4. Pour the honey lime glaze over the tilapia fillets. Secure the lid, set the vent to 'Sealing', and select 'Steam' for 4 minutes.
5. Perform a quick release once done, and carefully remove the tilapia. Serve hot, garnished with fresh cilantro or parsley if desired.

Nutritional Information: 220 calories, 28g protein, 15g carbohydrates, 6g fat, 0g fiber, 60mg cholesterol, 180mg sodium, 460mg potassium.

Creamy Lobster & Corn Soup

Yield: 4 servings | Prep time: 15 minutes | Cook time: 20 minutes

Ingredients:

- 2 lobster tails, meat removed and chopped
- 2 cups corn kernels, fresh or frozen
- 1 medium onion, diced
- 2 garlic cloves, minced
- 3 cups low-sodium vegetable or seafood broth
- 1 cup light coconut milk or unsweetened almond milk
- 1 tsp olive oil
- 1/4 tsp black pepper
- 1/4 tsp salt (optional for DASH)
- 1 tbsp fresh parsley, chopped (for garnish)
- 1 green onion, thinly sliced (for garnish)

Directions:

1. Set the Instant Pot on 'Sauté' mode. Once hot, add olive oil, onion, and garlic. Sauté until onion is translucent.
2. Add corn kernels, lobster meat, broth, salt (if using), and pepper. Stir well.
3. Secure the lid, set the vent to 'Sealing', and select 'Soup' mode for 15 minutes.
4. Once done, perform a quick release. Stir in the coconut milk or almond milk, and let it heat through for about 2 minutes without boiling.
5. Serve hot, garnished with fresh parsley and green onion.

Nutritional Information: 260 calories, 20g protein, 25g carbohydrates, 8g fat, 3g fiber, 70mg cholesterol, 280mg sodium, 620mg potassium.

Teriyaki Glazed Tuna Steaks

Yield: 4 servings | Prep time: 10 minutes | Cook time: 8 minutes

Ingredients:

- 4 tuna steaks, about 6 oz each
- 1/4 cup low-sodium soy sauce
- 2 tbsp honey
- 1 tbsp rice vinegar
- 1 garlic clove, minced

- 1 tsp fresh ginger, grated
- 1 tbsp olive oil
- 1 tbsp water
- 2 tsp cornstarch
- Sesame seeds and sliced green onions, for garnish

Directions:

1. In a bowl, whisk together the soy sauce, honey, rice vinegar, garlic, and ginger. Pour half of the mixture over the tuna steaks and let them marinate for 5 minutes.
2. Set the Instant Pot to 'Sauté' mode. Once hot, add the olive oil and sear the tuna steaks for 1 minute on each side. Remove and set aside.
3. In the pot, add the remaining teriyaki sauce mixture. Combine water and cornstarch in a small bowl and stir into the sauce to thicken it slightly.
4. Place the tuna steaks back into the Instant Pot, coat them with the sauce, and let them simmer for 2-3 minutes.
5. Serve the tuna steaks hot with sauce drizzled over, garnished with sesame seeds and green onions.

Nutritional Information:240 calories, 35g protein, 12g carbohydrates, 4g fat, 0g fiber, 60mg cholesterol, 320mg sodium, 480mg potassium.

Mediterranean Sea Bass with Tomatoes

Yield: 4 servings | Prep time: 15 minutes | Cook time: 8 minutes

Ingredients:

- 4 sea bass fillets, about 6 oz each
- 1 cup cherry tomatoes, halved
- 3 garlic cloves, minced
- 1/4 cup Kalamata olives, pitted and sliced
- 1/4 cup fresh basil, chopped

- 1/4 cup low-sodium vegetable broth
- 2 tbsp olive oil
- Zest and juice of 1 lemon
- Salt and pepper, to taste

Directions:

1. Season the sea bass fillets with salt, pepper, and half of the lemon zest.
2. Set the Instant Pot to 'Sauté' mode. Add olive oil and once hot, place the fillets skin-side down, cooking for about 2 minutes until they develop a light crust. Remove and set aside.
3. In the pot, add garlic and sauté briefly. Then add tomatoes, olives, and vegetable broth, stirring to combine.
4. Place the sea bass fillets back into the Instant Pot. Drizzle with lemon juice and sprinkle with remaining lemon zest.
5. Close the lid and set the Instant Pot to 'Manual' or 'Pressure Cook' mode for 6 minutes. Once done, quick release the pressure. Serve the fillets with the tomato mixture, garnishing with fresh basil.

Nutritional Information:280 calories, 30g protein, 6g carbohydrates, 15g fat, 2g fiber, 70mg cholesterol, 260mg sodium, 450mg potassium.

Garlic Butter Poached Scallops

Yield: 4 servings | Prep time: 10 minutes | Cook time: 4 minutes

Ingredients:

- 16 large sea scallops, cleaned and muscle removed
- 4 garlic cloves, minced
- 3 tbsp unsalted butter, melted
- 1 cup low-sodium vegetable broth
- 1 tbsp fresh parsley, chopped
- Zest of 1 lemon
- Salt and pepper, to taste
- 1 tsp olive oil (for sautéing)

Directions:

1. Season the scallops with salt and pepper.
2. Set the Instant Pot to 'Sauté' mode. Add olive oil and garlic, sautéing briefly until fragrant.
3. Add the melted butter and vegetable broth into the pot and stir.
4. Carefully place the scallops into the Instant Pot. Close the lid and set the Instant Pot to 'Low Pressure' or 'Pressure Cook' mode for 2 minutes.
5. Once done, quick release the pressure. Serve the scallops drizzled with the garlic butter sauce, sprinkled with lemon zest and fresh parsley.

Nutritional Information: 190 calories, 15g protein, 5g carbohydrates, 12g fat, 0g fiber, 50mg cholesterol, 250mg sodium, 350mg potassium.

Wholesome Whole Grain & Pasta Plates

Farro Risotto with Asparagus & Lemon

Yield: 4 servings | Prep time: 15 minutes | Cook time: 25 minutes

Ingredients:

- 1 cup farro, rinsed and drained
- 2 cups low-sodium vegetable broth
- 1 tbsp olive oil
- 1 small onion, finely chopped
- 2 garlic cloves, minced
- 1 bunch asparagus, trimmed and cut into 1-inch pieces
- Zest and juice of 1 lemon
- 1/4 cup grated Parmesan cheese (optional for added flavor, but consider sodium content)
- Salt and pepper, to taste
- 2 tbsp fresh parsley, chopped

Directions:

1. Set the Instant Pot to 'Sauté' mode. Add olive oil, onion, and garlic. Sauté until the onions are translucent.
2. Add the farro to the pot and stir for a minute. Pour in the vegetable broth.
3. Close the Instant Pot lid and set to 'Manual' or 'Pressure Cook' on high pressure for 20 minutes.
4. Once done, quick release the pressure. Stir in the asparagus, lemon zest, and lemon juice. Allow the residual heat to cook the asparagus slightly, keeping it crisp.
5. Season with salt, pepper, and stir in parsley. If using, sprinkle with Parmesan cheese before serving.

Nutritional Information:230 calories, 8g protein, 45g carbohydrates, 3g fat, 8g fiber, 5mg cholesterol, 150mg sodium, 280mg potassium.

Whole Wheat Spaghetti with Fresh Tomato Sauce

Yield: 4 servings | Prep time: 10 minutes | Cook time: 20 minutes

Ingredients:

- 8 oz whole wheat spaghetti
- 2 tbsp olive oil
- 3 garlic cloves, minced
- 1 small onion, diced
- 2 1/2 cups fresh tomatoes, chopped
- 1/2 cup low-sodium vegetable broth
- 2 tbsp fresh basil, chopped
- 2 tbsp fresh parsley, chopped
- Salt and pepper, to taste
- 1/4 cup grated Parmesan cheese (optional for added flavor, but consider sodium content)
- Red pepper flakes (optional)

Directions:

1. Set the Instant Pot to 'Sauté' mode. Add olive oil, garlic, and onions. Sauté until onions are translucent.
2. Add the fresh tomatoes, vegetable broth, salt, and pepper. Stir well.
3. Break the spaghetti in half and add to the pot, ensuring it is submerged in the sauce.
4. Lock the Instant Pot lid and set it to 'Manual' or 'Pressure Cook' on high pressure for 8 minutes. Once completed, quick release the pressure.
5. Stir in fresh basil, parsley, and optionally add red pepper flakes for a bit of heat. If using, sprinkle with Parmesan cheese before serving.

Nutritional Information:330 calories, 12g protein, 58g carbohydrates, 7g fat, 10g fiber, 5mg cholesterol, 100mg sodium, 350mg potassium.

Mediterranean Quinoa Salad

Yield: 4 servings | Prep time: 15 minutes | Cook time: 15 minutes

Ingredients:

- 1 cup quinoa, rinsed and drained
- 1 1/2 cups low-sodium vegetable broth
- 1/2 cup cherry tomatoes, halved
- 1/2 cup cucumber, diced
- 1/3 cup Kalamata olives, sliced
- 1/4 cup red onion, finely chopped

- 1/4 cup feta cheese, crumbled (optional, consider sodium content)
- 2 tbsp olive oil
- 2 tbsp lemon juice
- 1 tbsp fresh parsley, chopped
- 1 tbsp fresh mint, chopped
- Salt and pepper, to taste

Directions:

1. Add quinoa and vegetable broth to the Instant Pot. Lock the lid and set the Instant Pot to 'Manual' or 'Pressure Cook' on high for 1 minute. Once completed, allow a natural release for 10 minutes, then perform a quick release.
2. Transfer the cooked quinoa to a large mixing bowl and let it cool for a few minutes.
3. To the cooled quinoa, add cherry tomatoes, cucumber, olives, red onion, and feta cheese.
4. In a separate small bowl, whisk together olive oil, lemon juice, parsley, mint, salt, and pepper. Pour the dressing over the quinoa mixture and toss to combine.
5. Serve immediately or refrigerate for later use.

Nutritional Information:310 calories, 10g protein, 42g carbohydrates, 13g fat, 5g fiber, 8mg cholesterol, 250mg sodium, 400mg potassium.

Orzo with Spinach, Feta & Olives

Yield: 4 servings | Prep time: 10 minutes | Cook time: 8 minutes

Ingredients:

- 1 cup uncooked orzo pasta
- 2 cups low-sodium vegetable broth
- 2 cups fresh spinach, roughly chopped
- 1/2 cup feta cheese, crumbled (consider sodium content)
- 1/4 cup Kalamata olives, pitted and sliced

- 2 tbsp olive oil
- 2 garlic cloves, minced
- 1/2 lemon, zest and juice
- Salt and pepper, to taste
- Fresh parsley, chopped for garnish

Directions:

1. Set the Instant Pot to 'Sauté' mode and heat the olive oil. Add garlic and sauté for about 1 minute until fragrant.
2. Add orzo and vegetable broth to the Instant Pot. Lock the lid and set the Instant Pot to 'Manual' or 'Pressure Cook' on high for 4 minutes.
3. Once completed, allow a natural release for 2 minutes, then perform a quick release.
4. Stir in spinach, allowing it to wilt from the heat. Mix in feta cheese, olives, lemon zest, lemon juice, and season with salt and pepper.
5. Serve immediately, garnished with fresh parsley.

Nutritional Information:265 calories, 8g protein, 35g carbohydrates, 10g fat, 3g fiber, 15mg cholesterol, 350mg sodium, 230mg potassium.

Brown Rice & Veggie Stir Fry

Yield: 4 servings | Prep time: 15 minutes | Cook time: 22 minutes

Ingredients:

- 1 cup brown rice, rinsed and drained
- 2 1/4 cups low-sodium vegetable broth
- 2 tbsp olive oil
- 1 medium onion, sliced
- 1 bell pepper, sliced
- 2 medium carrots, julienned
- 1 cup broccoli florets
- 2 garlic cloves, minced
- 2 tbsp low-sodium soy sauce
- 1 tbsp sesame oil
- 1 tsp grated ginger
- 2 green onions, sliced for garnish
- 1 tbsp sesame seeds for garnish

Directions:

1. In the Instant Pot, combine brown rice and vegetable broth. Lock the lid, set the vent to 'Sealing', and pressure cook on high for 20 minutes. Once done, allow natural pressure release for 10 minutes.
2. Using a different pan or after transferring cooked rice to a bowl, set the Instant Pot to 'Sauté' mode and add olive oil. Add onions, bell pepper, carrots, and broccoli. Sauté for 3-4 minutes until slightly softened.
3. Add garlic and ginger, sautéing for another minute. Mix in cooked rice.
4. Drizzle with low-sodium soy sauce and sesame oil, stirring to combine. Cook for 2 more minutes.
5. Serve garnished with green onions and sesame seeds.

Nutritional Information: 295 calories, 7g protein, 49g carbohydrates, 8g fat, 5g fiber, 0mg cholesterol, 220mg sodium, 390mg potassium.

Barley & Vegetable Casserole

Yield: 4 servings | Prep time: 15 minutes | Cook time: 25 minutes

Ingredients:

- 1 cup pearled barley, rinsed and drained
- 2 1/2 cups low-sodium vegetable broth
- 1 tbsp olive oil
- 1 medium onion, diced
- 2 garlic cloves, minced
- 1 zucchini, diced
- 1 bell pepper, diced
- 1 cup diced tomatoes (canned or fresh)
- 1 tsp dried oregano
- 1 tsp dried basil
- Salt and pepper to taste
- 1/4 cup grated parmesan cheese (optional)
- Fresh parsley, chopped for garnish

Directions:

1. In the Instant Pot, set to 'Sauté' mode and add olive oil. Sauté onions and garlic until translucent.
2. Add zucchini, bell pepper, and tomatoes, cooking for another 2-3 minutes.
3. Stir in barley, dried oregano, dried basil, salt, and pepper. Pour in the vegetable broth.
4. Lock the lid, set the vent to 'Sealing', and pressure cook on high for 20 minutes. Allow natural pressure release for 5 minutes.
5. If desired, stir in parmesan cheese while hot. Serve garnished with fresh parsley.

Nutritional Information: 280 calories, 8g protein, 54g carbohydrates, 4g fat, 11g fiber, 5mg cholesterol, 180mg sodium, 370mg potassium.

Penne with Eggplant & Ricotta

Yield: 4 servings | Prep time: 15 minutes | Cook time: 10 minutes

Ingredients:

- 8 oz whole wheat penne
- 1 tbsp olive oil
- 1 medium-sized eggplant, diced into 1-inch pieces
- 3 garlic cloves, minced
- 1 cup low-sodium canned crushed tomatoes
- 1/2 tsp dried basil
- 1/2 tsp dried oregano
- Salt and pepper to taste
- 3/4 cup low-fat ricotta cheese
- 1/4 cup fresh parsley, chopped
- 1/4 cup grated parmesan cheese (optional for garnish)

Directions:

1. Set the Instant Pot to 'Sauté' mode and add olive oil. Sauté garlic for 1 minute, then add diced eggplant. Cook until eggplant softens, about 3-4 minutes.
2. Stir in crushed tomatoes, dried basil, dried oregano, salt, and pepper. Mix thoroughly.
3. Add penne to the mixture and pour enough water to just cover the pasta.
4. Lock the lid, set the vent to 'Sealing', and pressure cook on high for 6 minutes. Quick release the pressure.
5. Stir in ricotta cheese until creamy and well combined. Serve garnished with parsley and optional parmesan.

Nutritional Information:320 calories, 14g protein, 56g carbohydrates, 5g fat, 10g fiber, 20mg cholesterol, 180mg sodium, 410mg potassium.

Three-Grain Pilaf with Almonds

Yield: 4 servings | Prep time: 10 minutes | Cook time: 20 minutes

Ingredients:

- 1/4 cup quinoa
- 1/4 cup brown rice
- 1/4 cup bulgur wheat
- 1 tbsp olive oil
- 1 small onion, finely chopped
- 2 cups low-sodium vegetable broth
- 1/2 cup slivered almonds, toasted
- Salt and pepper to taste
- 2 tbsp fresh parsley, chopped
- 1 tsp lemon zest

Directions:

1. Set the Instant Pot to 'Sauté' mode. Add olive oil and sauté the chopped onion until translucent.
2. Add the quinoa, brown rice, and bulgur wheat. Stir and sauté for 2-3 minutes until the grains are slightly toasted.
3. Pour in the vegetable broth. Season with salt and pepper.
4. Lock the lid, set the vent to 'Sealing', and pressure cook on high for 15 minutes. Allow a natural pressure release for 5 minutes before performing a quick release.
5. Fluff the pilaf with a fork. Mix in toasted almonds, lemon zest, and fresh parsley before serving.

Nutritional Information:260 calories, 8g protein, 40g carbohydrates, 9g fat, 6g fiber, 0mg cholesterol, 150mg sodium, 270mg potassium.

Buckwheat Noodles with Sesame Vegetables

Yield: 4 servings | Prep time: 15 minutes | Cook time: 5 minutes

Ingredients:

- 8 oz buckwheat noodles (soba)
- 1 tbsp olive oil
- 2 cloves garlic, minced
- 1 medium carrot, julienned
- 1 bell pepper, sliced thin
- 1 zucchini, julienned
- 2 tbsp low-sodium soy sauce
- 1 tbsp sesame oil
- 2 tbsp toasted sesame seeds
- 2 green onions, sliced
- Salt and pepper to taste

Directions:

1. Cook the buckwheat noodles as per package instructions, then drain and set aside.
2. Set the Instant Pot to 'Sauté' mode. Add olive oil, garlic, carrot, bell pepper, and zucchini. Sauté for about 3 minutes or until vegetables are slightly softened.
3. Add the cooked noodles, low-sodium soy sauce, and sesame oil. Stir to combine and let cook for an additional 1-2 minutes.
4. Turn off the Instant Pot. Sprinkle the dish with toasted sesame seeds, green onions, salt, and pepper. Toss gently and serve.

Nutritional Information: 260 calories, 9g protein, 45g carbohydrates, 6g fat, 5g fiber, 0mg cholesterol, 240mg sodium, 290mg potassium.

Creamy Mushroom & Wild Rice Soup

Yield: 4 servings | Prep time: 10 minutes | Cook time: 30 minutes

Ingredients:

- 1 cup wild rice, rinsed
- 2 tbsp olive oil
- 1 medium onion, diced
- 3 cloves garlic, minced
- 1 pound mixed fresh mushrooms, sliced (e.g., button, cremini, shiitake)
- 4 cups low-sodium vegetable broth
- 1 cup water
- 1 tsp dried thyme
- 1 tsp dried rosemary
- Salt and pepper to taste
- 1/2 cup low-fat Greek yogurt
- 2 tbsp fresh parsley, chopped

Directions:

1. Set the Instant Pot to 'Sauté' mode. Add olive oil, onion, and garlic. Sauté for 3 minutes until onions are translucent. Add mushrooms and continue to sauté for another 5 minutes.
2. Add the wild rice, vegetable broth, water, thyme, rosemary, salt, and pepper to the pot. Stir to combine.
3. Close the lid of the Instant Pot, set the valve to 'Sealing', and cook on 'High Pressure' for 25 minutes.
4. Quick release the pressure. Stir in the Greek yogurt to give the soup a creamy texture. Adjust seasoning if necessary.
5. Serve the soup hot, garnished with fresh parsley.

Nutritional Information: 230 calories, 8g protein, 40g carbohydrates, 5g fat, 4g fiber, 3mg cholesterol, 250mg sodium 380mg potassium.

Spelt Berry Salad with Roasted Veggies

Yield: 4 servings | Prep time: 15 minutes | Cook time: 25 minutes

Ingredients:

- 1 cup spelt berries, rinsed and drained
- 2 1/2 cups water
- 1 tbsp olive oil
- 2 cups mixed vegetables (bell peppers, zucchini, and cherry tomatoes), diced
- 1/4 cup fresh basil, chopped
- 2 tbsp fresh lemon juice
- 1 tbsp balsamic vinegar
- 2 garlic cloves, minced
- Salt and pepper to taste
- 1/4 cup feta cheese, crumbled (optional)

Directions:

1. Place spelt berries and water in the Instant Pot. Close the lid, set the valve to 'Sealing', and cook on 'High Pressure' for 20 minutes. Allow natural release for 10 minutes before quick releasing the remaining pressure.
2. Set Instant Pot to 'Sauté' mode. Add olive oil and the diced vegetables. Sauté for 5 minutes or until the vegetables are tender but still crisp.
3. In a separate bowl, whisk together lemon juice, balsamic vinegar, garlic, salt, and pepper. Pour this dressing over the cooked spelt berries and vegetables. Stir well to combine.
4. Allow the salad to cool slightly. Mix in the fresh basil and top with crumbled feta cheese before serving.

Nutritional Information: 250 calories, 9g protein, 42g carbohydrates, 6g fat, 8g fiber, 5mg cholesterol, 180mg sodium, 320mg potassium.

Millet & Lentil Stuffed Peppers

Yield: 4 servings | Prep time: 20 minutes | Cook time: 25 minutes

Ingredients:

- 4 large bell peppers (any color), tops removed and seeds discarded
- 1 cup millet, rinsed and drained
- 1/2 cup green lentils, rinsed and drained
- 2 1/2 cups vegetable broth
- 1 small onion, finely chopped
- 2 garlic cloves, minced
- 1 tbsp olive oil
- 1 tsp smoked paprika
- 1 tsp ground cumin
- Salt and pepper to taste
- 1/4 cup fresh parsley, chopped (for garnish)

Directions:

1. Set Instant Pot to 'Sauté' mode. Add olive oil, onion, and garlic. Sauté until onion is translucent. Add millet, lentils, smoked paprika, cumin, salt, and pepper. Stir well.
2. Pour in the vegetable broth and stir again. Nestle the bell peppers into the mixture.
3. Close the Instant Pot lid, set the valve to 'Sealing', and cook on 'High Pressure' for 15 minutes. Allow natural release for 10 minutes, then perform a quick release.
4. Carefully remove the peppers from the Instant Pot. They should be tender and filled with the millet-lentil mixture.
5. Garnish with fresh parsley before serving.

Nutritional Information: 275 calories, 10g protein, 50g carbohydrates, 4g fat, 9g fiber, 0mg cholesterol, 200mg sodium, 400mg potassium.

Lasagna with Spinach & Ricotta

Yield: 6 servings | Prep time: 30 minutes | Cook time: 40 minutes

Ingredients:

- 12 whole wheat lasagna noodles
- 2 cups fresh spinach, chopped
- 2 cups ricotta cheese (low-fat)
- 1/4 cup grated Parmesan cheese
- 1 egg, lightly beaten
- 3 cups tomato sauce (low-sodium)
- 2 garlic cloves, minced
- 1 tsp dried oregano
- 1 tsp dried basil
- Salt and pepper to taste
- 1 cup shredded mozzarella cheese (low-fat)
- 1 tbsp olive oil

Directions:

1. In a bowl, mix together ricotta cheese, Parmesan, egg, spinach, salt, and pepper. Set aside.
2. Spread 1 cup of tomato sauce at the bottom of the Instant Pot. Place a layer of lasagna noodles, breaking them if needed to fit.
3. Spread a portion of the ricotta mixture over the noodles, followed by a sprinkle of mozzarella and a portion of the tomato sauce mixed with garlic, oregano, and basil.
4. Repeat layers until all ingredients are used, finishing with a layer of tomato sauce and mozzarella on top.
5. Close the Instant Pot lid, set the valve to 'Sealing', and cook on 'Manual' or 'Pressure Cook' mode on 'Low' for 40 minutes. Allow natural release.

Nutritional Information:350 calories, 18g protein, 45g carbohydrates, 10g fat, 6g fiber, 50mg cholesterol, 280mg sodium, 600mg potassium.

Farfalle with Pesto, Peas & Pine Nuts

Yield: 6 servings | Prep time: 15 minutes | Cook time: 8 minutes

Ingredients:

- 2 cups whole wheat farfalle (bow-tie pasta)
- 1 cup fresh basil leaves
- 1/4 cup pine nuts, toasted
- 2 garlic cloves
- 1/4 cup grated Parmesan cheese
- 2 tbsp olive oil
- 1 cup fresh peas (or frozen and thawed)
- Salt and pepper to taste
- 1/4 cup water
- 1 tbsp lemon juice
- 1/4 cup low-sodium vegetable broth

Directions:

1. In a blender or food processor, combine basil, pine nuts, garlic, Parmesan cheese, olive oil, lemon juice, salt, and pepper. Blend until smooth to make the pesto sauce. Set aside.
2. Add vegetable broth and water to the Instant Pot. Stir in the farfalle pasta.
3. Close the Instant Pot lid, set the valve to 'Sealing', and cook on 'Manual' or 'Pressure Cook' mode on 'High' for 4 minutes. Quick release the pressure.
4. Add peas to the pot and stir well. Let the residual heat cook the peas for about 2-3 minutes.
5. Finally, mix in the pesto sauce until well combined. Garnish with additional pine nuts and serve immediately.

Nutritional Information:380 calories, 12g protein, 52g carbohydrates, 14g fat, 8g fiber, 5mg cholesterol, 140mg sodium, 350mg potassium.

Red Rice & Vegetable Medley

Yield: 6 servings | Prep time: 15 minutes | Cook time: 25 minutes

Ingredients:

- 1 1/2 cups red rice, rinsed and drained
- 2 1/2 cups low-sodium vegetable broth
- 1 medium zucchini, diced
- 1 medium bell pepper (color of choice), diced
- 1 medium carrot, diced
- 1/2 cup green beans, chopped
- 1/2 cup fresh or frozen corn kernels
- 1 small onion, finely chopped
- 2 garlic cloves, minced
- 1 tbsp olive oil
- Salt and pepper to taste
- 2 tbsp fresh parsley, chopped (for garnish)

Directions:

1. Set the Instant Pot to "Sauté" mode and heat the olive oil. Add onions and garlic, and sauté until translucent.
2. Add zucchini, bell pepper, carrot, green beans, and corn to the pot. Stir well and sauté for an additional 3 minutes.
3. Add red rice to the pot along with vegetable broth, salt, and pepper. Mix everything together.
4. Close the Instant Pot lid, set the valve to 'Sealing', and cook on 'Manual' or 'Pressure Cook' mode on 'High' for 20 minutes. Allow for a natural pressure release for 10 minutes, then quick release the remaining pressure.
5. Fluff the rice with a fork, adjust seasonings if necessary, garnish with fresh parsley, and serve.

Nutritional Information: 220 calories, 5g protein, 44g carbohydrates, 3g fat, 4g fiber, 0mg cholesterol, 100mg sodium, 290mg potassium.

Vivacious Vegetables & Side Dishes

Garlic Parmesan Brussels Sprouts

Yield: 4 servings | Prep time: 10 minutes | Cook time: 5 minutes

Ingredients:

- 1 lb Brussels sprouts, trimmed and halved
- 4 cloves garlic, minced
- 1 tbsp olive oil
- 1/4 cup grated Parmesan cheese
- 1/4 cup water or low-sodium vegetable broth
- Salt and pepper to taste
- 1 tbsp fresh lemon juice
- 1 tsp lemon zest
- 2 tbsp fresh parsley, chopped (for garnish)

Directions:

1. Set the Instant Pot to "Sauté" mode and heat the olive oil. Add garlic and sauté for 1 minute until fragrant.
2. Add Brussels sprouts, water or broth, salt, and pepper to the pot, stirring well.
3. Close the Instant Pot lid, set the valve to 'Sealing', and cook on 'Manual' or 'Pressure Cook' mode on 'High' for 2 minutes. Quick release the pressure after the cooking cycle completes.
4. Open the lid and stir in lemon juice, lemon zest, and grated Parmesan cheese. Adjust seasonings if necessary.
5. Serve in a bowl, garnished with fresh parsley.

Nutritional Information: 95 calories, 6g protein, 11g carbohydrates, 4g fat, 4g fiber, 7mg cholesterol, 150mg sodium, 450mg potassium.

Honey Glazed Carrots

Yield: 4 servings | Prep time: 10 minutes | Cook time: 5 minutes

Ingredients:

- 1 lb baby carrots, washed and trimmed
- 2 tbsp honey
- 1 tbsp olive oil
- 1/4 cup water
- Pinch of salt
- 1 tsp fresh thyme (optional)
- 1 tbsp lemon juice
- 1 tbsp fresh parsley, chopped (for garnish)

Directions:

1. Place baby carrots, water, and a pinch of salt into the Instant Pot.
2. Close the Instant Pot lid, set the valve to 'Sealing', and cook on 'Manual' or 'Pressure Cook' mode on 'High' for 3 minutes. Quick release the pressure once the cooking cycle completes.
3. Set the Instant Pot to "Sauté" mode and stir in honey and olive oil. Sauté for about 2 minutes or until carrots are well-coated and slightly caramelized. Stir in thyme if using.
4. Turn off the Instant Pot, drizzle carrots with lemon juice, and give a final stir.
5. Serve the carrots garnished with fresh parsley.

Nutritional Information: 90 calories, 1g protein, 18g carbohydrates, 2.5g fat, 3g fiber, 0mg cholesterol, 85mg sodium, 350mg potassium.

Creamy Cauliflower Mash

Yield: 4 servings | Prep time: 10 minutes | Cook time: 8 minutes

Ingredients:

- 1 large head of cauliflower, cut into florets
- 3/4 cup water
- 2 cloves garlic, minced
- 2 tbsp olive oil or unsalted butter
- 1/4 cup unsweetened almond milk (or any unsweetened milk of choice)
- Salt to taste (keeping it minimal for DASH)
- Freshly ground black pepper, to taste
- 1 tbsp fresh chives or parsley, chopped (optional for garnish)

Directions:

1. Place cauliflower florets, garlic, and water into the Instant Pot.
2. Secure the lid, set the valve to 'Sealing', and select 'Manual' or 'Pressure Cook' mode on 'High' for 5 minutes. Once done, quick release the pressure.
3. Drain any excess water from the pot and add olive oil or butter, and almond milk to the cauliflower.
4. Using an immersion blender or a potato masher, puree the cauliflower until smooth and creamy. Season with salt and pepper according to your preference.
5. Serve in bowls, garnishing with chives or parsley if desired.

Nutritional Information:
105 calories, 3g protein, 12g carbohydrates, 6g fat, 5g fiber, 0mg cholesterol, 80mg sodium, 450mg potassium.

Slow Cooked Ratatouille

Yield: 4 servings | Prep time: 20 minutes | Cook time: 45 minutes

Ingredients:

- 1 medium eggplant, diced into 1-inch cubes
- 2 medium zucchinis, sliced
- 1 large red bell pepper, diced
- 1 large yellow onion, thinly sliced
- 3 medium tomatoes, diced
- 4 cloves garlic, minced
- 2 tbsp olive oil
- 1 tsp dried basil
- 1 tsp dried thyme
- Salt to taste (keeping it minimal for DASH)
- Freshly ground black pepper, to taste
- 2 tbsp fresh parsley or basil, chopped (for garnish)
- 1/4 cup water

Directions:

1. In the Instant Pot, combine eggplant, zucchinis, bell pepper, onion, tomatoes, and garlic. Drizzle with olive oil and sprinkle with dried basil, thyme, salt, and pepper.
2. Add water to the mixture to help steam and prevent sticking.
3. Secure the lid, set the pot to 'Slow Cook' mode, and cook on 'Low' for 45 minutes or until the vegetables are tender and flavors melded.
4. Once cooked, adjust seasoning if necessary, and give it a gentle stir.
5. Serve warm, garnished with fresh parsley or basil.

Nutritional Information: 130 calories, 3g protein, 20g carbohydrates, 5g fat, 6g fiber, 0mg cholesterol, 50mg sodium, 600mg potassium.

Spiced Sweet Potato Wedges

Yield: 4 servings | Prep time: 10 minutes | Cook time: 15 minutes

Ingredients:

- 2 large sweet potatoes, washed and cut into wedges
- 1 tbsp olive oil
- 1/2 tsp smoked paprika
- 1/4 tsp ground cumin
- 1/4 tsp ground cinnamon
- 1/8 tsp cayenne pepper (optional for extra heat)
- Salt to taste (minimal for DASH)
- Freshly ground black pepper, to taste
- 1 cup water
- Fresh parsley or cilantro, chopped (for garnish)

Directions:

1. In a large bowl, mix the sweet potato wedges with olive oil, smoked paprika, cumin, cinnamon, cayenne, salt, and black pepper until well coated.
2. Pour water into the Instant Pot, followed by a steamer basket or the metal trivet that came with your pot. Arrange the seasoned sweet potato wedges on the basket or trivet.
3. Secure the lid and set the pot to 'Pressure Cook' or 'Manual' on high for 7 minutes. Once done, do a quick release.
4. Gently remove the wedges from the Instant Pot and let them cool slightly before serving.
5. Garnish with fresh parsley or cilantro before serving.

Nutritional Information: 140 calories, 2g protein, 32g carbohydrates, 3.5g fat, 5g fiber, 0mg cholesterol, 70mg sodium, 450mg potassium.

Green Bean Almondine

Yield: 4 servings | Prep time: 10 minutes | Cook time: 6 minutes

Ingredients:

- 1 lb fresh green beans, trimmed
- 2 tbsp olive oil
- 1/4 cup sliced almonds
- 2 cloves garlic, minced
- Zest of 1 lemon
- Juice of 1/2 lemon
- Salt to taste (minimal for DASH)
- Freshly ground black pepper, to taste
- 1 cup water

Directions:

1. Pour water into the Instant Pot. Place the green beans in a steamer basket or on the metal trivet that came with your pot.
2. Secure the lid and set the pot to 'Pressure Cook' or 'Manual' on high for 1 minute. Once done, do a quick release and remove the beans, draining any excess water.
3. Set the Instant Pot to 'Sauté' mode. Add olive oil, sliced almonds, and garlic. Sauté until the almonds are golden brown, about 4-5 minutes.
4. Add the cooked green beans back to the pot. Toss with the almond mixture, lemon zest, lemon juice, salt, and pepper until well combined.
5. Transfer to a serving dish and serve immediately.

Nutritional Information: 110 calories, 3g protein, 11g carbohydrates, 7g fat, 4g fiber, 0mg cholesterol, 80mg sodium, 250mg potassium.

Balsamic Glazed Beets

Yield: 4 servings | Prep time: 15 minutes | Cook time: 25 minutes

Ingredients:

- 1 lb fresh beets, peeled and sliced into 1/4-inch thick rounds
- 1/2 cup balsamic vinegar
- 2 tbsp honey (or to taste)
- 1 tbsp olive oil

- 1 cup water
- Salt to taste (minimal for DASH)
- Freshly ground black pepper, to taste
- Fresh parsley for garnish (optional)

Directions:

1. Pour water into the Instant Pot. Add the sliced beets into the pot, either directly or in a steamer basket.
2. Secure the lid and set the pot to 'Pressure Cook' or 'Manual' on high for 12 minutes. Once done, do a quick release and transfer the beets to a bowl, draining any excess water.
3. Set the Instant Pot to 'Sauté' mode. Add balsamic vinegar and honey, letting it simmer until it reduces to a thick glaze, around 10-12 minutes.
4. Turn off the Instant Pot. Add olive oil, salt, and pepper to the glaze. Add the cooked beets back into the pot and toss them in the glaze until well-coated.
5. Transfer to a serving dish, garnish with fresh parsley if desired, and serve immediately.

Nutritional Information: 145 calories, 2g protein, 30g carbohydrates, 3.5g fat, 4g fiber, 0mg cholesterol, 90mg sodium, 400mg potassium.

Mediterranean Stuffed Tomatoes

Yield: 4 servings | Prep time: 20 minutes | Cook time: 15 minutes

Ingredients:

- 4 large tomatoes
- 1 cup cooked quinoa
- 1/2 cup chopped spinach
- 1/4 cup crumbled feta cheese (ensure it's low in sodium)
- 1/4 cup Kalamata olives, pitted and chopped

- 2 tbsp fresh basil, chopped
- 1 tbsp olive oil
- 1 garlic clove, minced
- Salt to taste (minimal for DASH)
- Freshly ground black pepper, to taste
- 1 cup water (for Instant Pot steaming)

Directions:

1. Slice off the tops of the tomatoes and scoop out the insides to create a hollow center. Set aside.
2. In a bowl, combine quinoa, spinach, feta cheese, olives, basil, olive oil, garlic, salt, and pepper. Mix well to combine.
3. Carefully stuff each tomato with the quinoa mixture, pressing down gently to pack the filling.
4. Pour water into the Instant Pot. Place the stuffed tomatoes on a trivet or steamer basket inside the Instant Pot.
5. Secure the lid and set the pot to 'Pressure Cook' or 'Manual' on high for 3 minutes. Once done, do a quick release and carefully transfer the tomatoes to a serving dish.

Nutritional Information: 210 calories, 7g protein, 27g carbohydrates, 9g fat, 5g fiber, 8mg cholesterol, 120mg sodium, 500mg potassium.

Herb Roasted Root Vegetables

Yield: 4 servings | Prep time: 15 minutes | Cook time: 20 minutes

Ingredients:

- 2 medium carrots, peeled and cut into chunks
- 2 parsnips, peeled and cut into chunks
- 1 large sweet potato, peeled and cut into chunks
- 2 medium beets, peeled and cut into chunks
- 1 tbsp olive oil
- 2 tsp mixed dried herbs (such as rosemary, thyme, and oregano)
- Salt to taste (minimal for DASH)
- Freshly ground black pepper, to taste
- 1 cup water (for Instant Pot steaming)

Directions:

1. In a large mixing bowl, toss the root vegetables with olive oil, mixed herbs, salt, and pepper until well coated.
2. Pour water into the Instant Pot. Place the seasoned root vegetables on a trivet or steamer basket inside the Instant Pot.
3. Secure the lid and set the pot to 'Pressure Cook' or 'Manual' on high for 5 minutes. Once done, let the pressure release naturally for 5 minutes, then do a quick release.
4. Carefully transfer the root vegetables to a serving dish and serve warm.

Nutritional Information: 180 calories, 3g protein, 35g carbohydrates, 3.5g fat, 6g fiber, 0mg cholesterol, 85mg sodium, 650mg potassium.

Garlic & Lemon Asparagus

Yield: 4 servings | Prep time: 10 minutes | Cook time: 3 minutes

Ingredients:

- 1 lb fresh asparagus, trimmed
- 3 garlic cloves, minced
- Zest and juice from 1 lemon
- 1 tbsp olive oil
- Salt to taste (minimal for DASH)
- Freshly ground black pepper, to taste
- 1 cup water (for Instant Pot steaming)

Directions:

1. In a mixing bowl, toss the asparagus with garlic, lemon zest, olive oil, salt, and pepper.
2. Pour water into the Instant Pot. Place the seasoned asparagus on a trivet or steamer basket inside the Instant Pot.
3. Secure the lid and set the pot to 'Pressure Cook' or 'Manual' on high for 2 minutes. Once done, quickly release the pressure.
4. Transfer the asparagus to a serving plate, drizzle with fresh lemon juice, and serve immediately.

Nutritional Information: 50 calories, 3g protein, 7g carbohydrates, 2.5g fat, 3g fiber, 0mg cholesterol, 60mg sodium, 240mg potassium.

Buttery Corn on the Cob

Yield: 4 servings | Prep time: 5 minutes | Cook time: 4 minutes

Ingredients:

- 4 fresh corn on the cob, husked and cleaned
- 2 cups water
- 2 tbsp unsalted butter (use less for a lower-fat version)

- Salt to taste (minimal for DASH)
- Freshly ground black pepper, optional

Directions:

1. Pour water into the Instant Pot and insert the trivet or steamer basket.
2. Place the corn on the cob on the trivet or in the steamer basket.
3. Secure the lid and set the Instant Pot to 'Pressure Cook' or 'Manual' on high for 2 minutes. Once done, quickly release the pressure.
4. Remove the corn and while still hot, rub each cob with butter. Season with minimal salt and optional black pepper, then serve immediately.

Nutritional Information: 155 calories, 4g protein, 31g carbohydrates, 5g fat, 3g fiber, 15mg cholesterol, 20mg sodium, 260mg potassium.

Zucchini & Squash Ribbons

Yield: 4 servings | Prep time: 10 minutes | Cook time: 2 minutes

Ingredients:

- 2 medium zucchinis
- 2 medium yellow squashes
- 1 cup water
- 1 tbsp olive oil

- 1 garlic clove, minced
- Salt to taste (minimal for DASH)
- Freshly ground black pepper, optional
- Fresh lemon zest for garnish, optional

Directions:

1. Use a vegetable peeler to slice the zucchini and yellow squash lengthwise into thin ribbons.
2. Turn on the Instant Pot's 'Sauté' mode. Add olive oil and minced garlic, sautéing for about 1 minute until fragrant.
3. Add the zucchini and squash ribbons to the Instant Pot, gently stirring to coat with garlic and oil. Sauté for about 1 minute.
4. Add water, secure the lid, and set the Instant Pot to 'Pressure Cook' or 'Manual' on low for 1 minute. Once done, quickly release the pressure.
5. Season with minimal salt and optional black pepper. If desired, sprinkle with fresh lemon zest before serving.

Nutritional Information: 50 calories, 2g protein, 6g carbohydrates, 3g fat, 2g fiber, 0mg cholesterol, 10mg sodium, 300mg potassium.

Rosemary Red Potatoes

Yield: 4 servings | Prep time: 10 minutes | Cook time: 10 minutes

Ingredients:

- 1.5 pounds red potatoes, washed and quartered
- 1 cup water
- 2 tbsp olive oil
- 2 fresh rosemary sprigs, leaves removed and finely chopped
- 1 garlic clove, minced
- Salt to taste (minimal for DASH)
- Freshly ground black pepper, optional

Directions:

1. Add water to the Instant Pot, followed by the red potatoes.
2. Secure the lid, and set the Instant Pot to 'Pressure Cook' or 'Manual' on high for 8 minutes. Once done, quickly release the pressure.
3. Turn on the Instant Pot's 'Sauté' mode. Drizzle the olive oil over the potatoes, sprinkle the minced garlic and chopped rosemary, and gently toss to coat.
4. Sauté for about 2 minutes or until the potatoes are slightly golden. Season with minimal salt and optional black pepper.

Nutritional Information:150 calories, 3g protein, 28g carbohydrates, 3.5g fat, 3g fiber, 0mg cholesterol, 20mg sodium, 700mg potassium.

Spinach & Garlic Sauté

Yield: 4 servings | Prep time: 5 minutes | Cook time: 3 minutes

Ingredients:

- 1 pound fresh spinach, washed and drained
- 3 garlic cloves, minced
- 2 tablespoons olive oil
- 1/4 cup water
- Salt to taste (minimal for DASH)
- Freshly ground black pepper, optional
- A squeeze of fresh lemon juice (optional)

Directions:

1. Turn on the Instant Pot's 'Sauté' mode. Add the olive oil and wait until it's shimmering.
2. Add the minced garlic and sauté for about 1 minute or until fragrant.
3. Add the fresh spinach and water. Gently toss the spinach to coat with the garlic and oil.
4. Sauté for about 2 minutes or until the spinach is wilted. Season with minimal salt, optional pepper, and a squeeze of fresh lemon juice if desired.

Nutritional Information:65 calories, 3g protein, 4g carbohydrates, 5g fat, 2g fiber, 0mg cholesterol, 80mg sodium, 500mg potassium.

Savory Mushroom & Onion Gravy

Yield: 4 servings | Prep time: 10 minutes | Cook time: 15 minutes

Ingredients:

- 1 cup sliced white mushrooms
- 1 medium onion, thinly sliced
- 2 cloves garlic, minced
- 2 cups low-sodium vegetable broth
- 1 tablespoon olive oil

- 2 tablespoons whole wheat flour or cornstarch for gluten-free
- Fresh thyme and rosemary, finely chopped (about 1 teaspoon each)
- Salt to taste (minimal for DASH)
- Freshly ground black pepper, optional

Directions:

1. Set the Instant Pot to 'Sauté' mode. Add olive oil, and once hot, sauté the onions, mushrooms, and garlic until they soften and brown slightly, around 5 minutes.
2. Sprinkle the flour over the vegetables and stir for another 2 minutes.
3. Slowly pour in the low-sodium vegetable broth, stirring continuously to avoid any lumps from forming. Add the fresh thyme and rosemary.
4. Seal the Instant Pot and set it to 'Pressure Cook' on high for 10 minutes. Once done, release the pressure manually and season with minimal salt and optional pepper.

Nutritional Information: 50 calories, 2g protein, 7g carbohydrates, 2g fat, 1g fiber, 0mg cholesterol, 50mg sodium, 150mg potassium.

Beans, Legumes & Lentil Loves

Smoky Black Bean Soup

Yield: 4 servings | Prep time: 10 minutes | Cook time: 30 minutes

Ingredients:

- 2 cups dried black beans, soaked overnight and drained
- 1 medium onion, diced
- 2 cloves garlic, minced
- 1 red bell pepper, diced
- 1 tablespoon olive oil
- 1 teaspoon smoked paprika
- 4 cups low-sodium vegetable broth
- 1 bay leaf
- Salt to taste (minimal for DASH)
- Fresh cilantro, chopped, for garnish
- 1 lime, juiced

Directions:

1. Set the Instant Pot to 'Sauté' mode. Add olive oil, and once hot, sauté the onions, garlic, and bell pepper until softened, about 3 minutes. Add smoked paprika and stir for another minute.
2. Add the soaked black beans, bay leaf, and low-sodium vegetable broth to the Instant Pot.
3. Seal the Instant Pot and set it to 'Pressure Cook' on high for 25 minutes. Once done, release the pressure naturally for about 10 minutes, then manually release any remaining pressure.
4. Season with minimal salt. Serve hot with a sprinkle of fresh cilantro and a splash of lime juice.

Nutritional Information:
220 calories, 12g protein, 40g carbohydrates, 3g fat, 10g fiber, 0mg cholesterol, 150mg sodium, 650mg potassium.

Red Lentil & Coconut Curry

Yield: 4 servings | Prep time: 15 minutes | Cook time: 20 minutes

Ingredients:

- 1 cup red lentils, rinsed and drained
- 2 cups low-sodium vegetable broth
- 1 can (13.5 oz) lite coconut milk
- 1 medium onion, diced
- 3 cloves garlic, minced
- 1 tablespoon olive oil
- 1 tablespoon curry powder
- 1 teaspoon ground turmeric
- 1 teaspoon ground cumin
- 1/2 teaspoon ground ginger
- Salt to taste (minimal for DASH)
- Fresh cilantro, chopped, for garnish
- 1 lime, juiced

Directions:

1. Set the Instant Pot to 'Sauté' mode. Add olive oil, and once hot, sauté the onions and garlic until softened, about 3 minutes. Add curry powder, turmeric, cumin, and ginger, stirring for another minute until fragrant.
2. Add the rinsed red lentils, vegetable broth, and lite coconut milk to the Instant Pot, stirring to combine.
3. Seal the Instant Pot and set it to 'Pressure Cook' on high for 15 minutes. Once done, release the pressure naturally for about 10 minutes, then manually release any remaining pressure.
4. Season with minimal salt. Serve hot garnished with fresh cilantro and a splash of lime juice.

Nutritional Information:
260 calories, 11g protein, 35g carbohydrates, 7g fat, 8g fiber, 0mg cholesterol, 160mg sodium, 650mg potassium.

Chickpea & Spinach Stew

Yield: 4 servings | Prep time: 10 minutes | Cook time: 25 minutes

Ingredients:

- 2 cans (15 oz each) low-sodium chickpeas, rinsed and drained
- 4 cups fresh spinach, washed and roughly chopped
- 1 medium onion, diced
- 3 cloves garlic, minced
- 1 can (14.5 oz) low-sodium diced tomatoes
- 1 tablespoon olive oil
-
- 1 teaspoon ground cumin
- 1/2 teaspoon smoked paprika
- 1/4 teaspoon ground turmeric
- 2 cups low-sodium vegetable broth
- Salt to taste (minimal for DASH)
- Fresh lemon juice from 1 lemon
- Fresh cilantro, for garnish

Directions:

1. Set the Instant Pot to 'Sauté' mode. Add olive oil, and once hot, sauté the onions and garlic until translucent, about 3 minutes. Add cumin, paprika, and turmeric, stirring for another minute.
2. Add the chickpeas, diced tomatoes with their juices, and vegetable broth into the Instant Pot. Stir to combine.
3. Seal the Instant Pot and set to 'Pressure Cook' on high for 20 minutes. Once done, perform a quick release.
4. Stir in the fresh spinach and allow it to wilt in the hot stew. Season with minimal salt and finish with a squeeze of fresh lemon juice. Garnish with cilantro before serving.

Nutritional Information:310 calories, 14g protein, 53g carbohydrates, 6g fat, 12g fiber, 0mg cholesterol, 320mg sodium, 810mg potassium.

Bean & Quinoa Salad with Lime Vinaigrette

Yield: 4 servings | Prep time: 15 minutes | Cook time: 12 minutes

Ingredients:

- 1 cup quinoa, rinsed and drained
- 1 can (15 oz) low-sodium black beans, rinsed and drained
- 1 cup cherry tomatoes, halved
- 1 medium bell pepper, diced
- 1/4 cup fresh cilantro, chopped
- 2 limes, zested and juiced
- 2 tablespoons olive oil
- 1 garlic clove, minced
- Salt to taste (minimal for DASH)
- 1 cup water
- 1 avocado, diced (for garnish)
- 1 green onion, chopped (for garnish)

Directions:

1. Place quinoa and water into the Instant Pot. Seal and set to 'Pressure Cook' for 12 minutes. Allow natural pressure release, then fluff quinoa with a fork.
2. While the quinoa cooks, prepare the vinaigrette: In a small bowl, whisk together lime zest, lime juice, olive oil, minced garlic, and minimal salt.
3. Transfer cooked quinoa to a large salad bowl. Let it cool for a few minutes.
4. Add black beans, cherry tomatoes, bell pepper, and cilantro to the bowl with the quinoa. Drizzle with the vinaigrette and toss gently to combine.
5. Garnish with diced avocado and chopped green onion before serving.

Nutritional Information:360 calories, 12g protein, 53g carbohydrates, 12g fat, 11g fiber, 0mg cholesterol, 150mg sodium, 680mg potassium.

Lentil Shepherd's Pie

Yield: 4 servings | Prep time: 20 minutes | Cook time: 25 minutes

Ingredients:

- 1 cup dried green or brown lentils, rinsed and drained
- 2 1/2 cups water
- 4 medium russet potatoes, peeled and diced
- 1/2 cup low-fat milk
- 1 tablespoon olive oil
- 1 onion, diced
- 2 carrots, diced
- 2 cloves garlic, minced
- 1 cup frozen peas
- 2 teaspoons fresh rosemary, minced
- Salt to taste (minimal for DASH)
- 1/2 teaspoon black pepper
- 1/2 cup low-sodium vegetable broth

Directions:

1. In the Instant Pot, combine lentils and water. Set to 'Pressure Cook' on high for 15 minutes. Once done, release pressure naturally and drain any excess water.
2. In a separate pot, boil the potatoes until tender. Mash with low-fat milk until creamy, then season with minimal salt and black pepper.
3. On the Instant Pot's 'Sauté' mode, heat olive oil. Add onions, carrots, and garlic. Cook until soft, about 5 minutes. Add peas, rosemary, and cooked lentils, stirring to combine. Pour in the vegetable broth, allowing to simmer for a few minutes.
4. Flatten the lentil mixture evenly. Carefully spread the mashed potatoes over the top.
5. Place the lid on the Instant Pot, ensuring it's set to 'Venting'. Use the 'Slow Cook' mode and let the pie heat for about 10 minutes, allowing the flavors to meld.

Nutritional Information: 350 calories, 18g protein, 60g carbohydrates, 4g fat, 15g fiber, 5mg cholesterol, 120mg sodium, 750mg potassium.

White Bean & Kale Soup

Yield: 4 servings | Prep time: 15 minutes | Cook time: 25 minutes

Ingredients:

- 2 cans (15 oz each) white beans (cannellini or great northern), drained and rinsed
- 1 tablespoon olive oil
- 1 onion, diced
- 2 cloves garlic, minced
- 4 cups low-sodium vegetable broth
- 3 cups kale, stemmed and chopped
- 2 carrots, diced
- 2 celery stalks, diced
- 1/2 teaspoon dried thyme
- 1/2 teaspoon dried rosemary
- Salt to taste (minimal for DASH)
- Black pepper to taste
- 1 bay leaf
- Juice of half a lemon

Directions:

1. Set Instant Pot to 'Sauté' mode and heat olive oil. Add onions and garlic, and cook until onions are translucent.
2. Add carrots, celery, thyme, and rosemary to the pot. Cook for another 3-4 minutes.
3. Pour in the vegetable broth, beans, kale, bay leaf, and season with minimal salt and black pepper. Stir to combine.
4. Close the lid, set to 'Pressure Cook' or 'Manual' on high for 20 minutes. Allow to release pressure naturally.
5. Open the lid, remove the bay leaf, and stir in lemon juice before serving.

Nutritional Information: 230 calories, 14g protein, 40g carbohydrates, 3g fat, 9g fiber, 0mg cholesterol, 280mg sodium, 850mg potassium.

Chana Masala

Yield: 4 servings | Prep time: 15 minutes | Cook time: 40 minutes

Ingredients:

- 2 cups chickpeas, soaked overnight and drained
- 1 tablespoon olive oil
- 1 large onion, finely chopped
- 2 cloves garlic, minced
- 1-inch ginger, grated
- 2 cups low-sodium diced tomatoes (canned or fresh)
- 1/2 teaspoon ground turmeric
- 1 teaspoon ground cumin
- 1 teaspoon ground coriander
- 1/4 teaspoon cayenne pepper (adjust to taste)
- 1 teaspoon garam masala
- Salt to taste (minimal for DASH)
- Black pepper to taste
- 2 cups low-sodium vegetable broth or water
- Fresh cilantro, chopped (for garnish)

Directions:

1. Set Instant Pot to 'Sauté' mode and heat olive oil. Add onions, ginger, and garlic, and sauté until onions are translucent.
2. Add turmeric, cumin, coriander, cayenne pepper, and garam masala. Stir well for 2 minutes until spices are fragrant.
3. Add the soaked chickpeas, diced tomatoes, vegetable broth or water, and season with minimal salt and black pepper.
4. Close the lid, set to 'Pressure Cook' or 'Manual' on high for 35 minutes. Allow to release pressure naturally.
5. Open the lid, stir well, and garnish with fresh cilantro before serving.

Nutritional Information: 260 calories, 12g protein, 45g carbohydrates, 4g fat, 12g fiber, 0mg cholesterol, 300mg sodium, 720mg potassium.

Three Bean Vegetarian Chili

Yield: 4 servings | Prep time: 20 minutes | Cook time: 25 minutes

Ingredients:

- 1 tablespoon olive oil
- 1 large onion, diced
- 2 cloves garlic, minced
- 1 bell pepper, diced
- 1 zucchini, diced
- 1/2 cup kidney beans, drained and rinsed
- 1/2 cup black beans, drained and rinsed
- 1/2 cup pinto beans, drained and rinsed
- 1 can (14 oz) low-sodium diced tomatoes
- 2 cups low-sodium vegetable broth
- 2 teaspoons chili powder
- 1 teaspoon cumin
- 1 teaspoon paprika
- Salt to taste (minimal for DASH)
- Black pepper to taste
- Fresh cilantro, chopped (for garnish)

Directions:

1. Set the Instant Pot to 'Sauté' mode. Add olive oil, onion, garlic, bell pepper, and zucchini. Sauté for about 5 minutes or until vegetables are slightly softened.
2. Add kidney beans, black beans, pinto beans, diced tomatoes, vegetable broth, chili powder, cumin, paprika, salt, and black pepper. Stir well.
3. Lock the Instant Pot lid in place and set to 'Pressure Cook' or 'Manual' on high for 20 minutes.
4. Allow a natural pressure release for 5 minutes, then perform a quick release.
5. Serve hot and garnish with fresh cilantro.

Nutritional Information: 270 calories, 15g protein, 50g carbohydrates, 3g fat, 14g fiber, 0mg cholesterol, 300mg sodium, 900mg potassium.

Lentil & Sausage Stew

Yield: 4 servings | Prep time: 15 minutes | Cook time: 25 minutes

Ingredients:

- 1 tablespoon olive oil
- 2 chicken sausages (low-sodium variety), sliced
- 1 cup dried lentils, rinsed and drained
- 1 large onion, diced
- 2 cloves garlic, minced
- 2 carrots, diced
- 1 celery stalk, diced
- 4 cups low-sodium vegetable broth
- 1 can (14 oz) low-sodium diced tomatoes
- 1 bay leaf
- 1/2 teaspoon smoked paprika
- 1/2 teaspoon ground black pepper
- Fresh parsley, chopped (for garnish)

Directions:

1. Set the Instant Pot to 'Sauté' mode. Add olive oil, chicken sausages, onion, and garlic. Sauté for about 5 minutes or until onions are translucent and sausages are lightly browned.
2. Add lentils, carrots, celery, vegetable broth, diced tomatoes, bay leaf, smoked paprika, and black pepper. Stir to combine.
3. Lock the Instant Pot lid in place and set to 'Pressure Cook' or 'Manual' on high for 20 minutes.
4. Allow a natural pressure release for 5 minutes, then perform a quick release.
5. Discard the bay leaf, stir well, and serve hot garnished with fresh parsley.

Nutritional Information: 320 calories, 23g protein, 40g carbohydrates, 8g fat, 16g fiber, 45mg cholesterol, 350mg sodium, 720mg potassium.

Mediterranean Hummus Dip

Yield: 4 servings | Prep time: 10 minutes | Cook time: 50 minutes

Ingredients:

- 1 cup dried chickpeas, soaked overnight and drained
- 4 cups water
- 3 cloves garlic
- 1/4 cup tahini
- Juice of 1 lemon
- 2 tablespoons olive oil
- 1/2 teaspoon ground cumin
- Salt to taste (remember to use sparingly for DASH diet suitability)
- 1/4 teaspoon smoked paprika (for garnish)
- 2 tablespoons chopped parsley (for garnish)
- 2 tablespoons pitted and sliced Kalamata olives (for garnish)

Directions:

1. Add soaked chickpeas and water to the Instant Pot. Close the lid and set to 'Pressure Cook' or 'Manual' for 40 minutes.
2. Allow a natural pressure release. Once depressurized, drain chickpeas and reserve a bit of the cooking liquid.
3. Combine cooked chickpeas, garlic, tahini, lemon juice, olive oil, cumin, and salt in a blender or food processor. Add reserved cooking liquid, a tablespoon at a time, until the desired consistency is achieved.
4. Transfer hummus to a bowl and drizzle with a bit more olive oil. Garnish with smoked paprika, chopped parsley, and sliced olives.

Nutritional Information: 250 calories, 8g protein, 28g carbohydrates, 14g fat, 8g fiber, 0mg cholesterol, 150mg sodium, 300mg potassium.

Black-Eyed Peas & Greens

Yield: 4 servings | Prep time: 15 minutes | Cook time: 30 minutes

Ingredients:

- 1 cup dried black-eyed peas, soaked overnight and drained
- 3 cups vegetable broth (low sodium)
- 1 onion, diced
- 3 cloves garlic, minced
- 1 bunch of greens (kale, collard, or mustard), stems removed and roughly chopped
- 1 teaspoon olive oil
- 1/4 teaspoon smoked paprika
- 1/2 teaspoon ground cumin
- Salt and pepper to taste (use sparingly for DASH diet suitability)
- 1 bay leaf
- 1 tablespoon apple cider vinegar
- Red pepper flakes (optional, for added heat)

Directions:

1. Set the Instant Pot to 'Sauté' mode and add olive oil. Once heated, add diced onion and garlic, cooking until translucent.
2. Add the smoked paprika, cumin, black-eyed peas, bay leaf, and vegetable broth to the pot. Stir well.
3. Close the Instant Pot lid, set to 'Pressure Cook' or 'Manual' for 20 minutes.
4. Once cooking is complete, allow a natural pressure release. Remove the bay leaf and add the greens, stirring until they wilt in the heat of the peas. Mix in the apple cider vinegar and adjust seasoning if necessary.
5. Serve warm, sprinkled with red pepper flakes if desired.

Nutritional Information: 220 calories, 14g protein, 40g carbohydrates, 1g fat, 8g fiber, 0mg cholesterol, 150mg sodium, 600mg potassium.

Mung Bean & Vegetable Curry

Yield: 4 servings | Prep time: 20 minutes | Cook time: 25 minutes

Ingredients:

- 1 cup dried mung beans, soaked overnight and drained
- 3 cups low-sodium vegetable broth
- 1 onion, diced
- 2 cloves garlic, minced
- 1 carrot, diced
- 1 bell pepper, diced
- 1 zucchini, diced
- 2 tomatoes, diced
- 1 teaspoon olive oil
- 1/4 teaspoon ground turmeric
- 1/2 teaspoon ground cumin
- 1/4 teaspoon ground coriander
- 1/2 teaspoon garam masala
- Salt and pepper to taste (use sparingly for DASH diet suitability)
- Fresh cilantro for garnish (optional)
- 1 tablespoon lemon juice

Directions:

1. Set the Instant Pot to 'Sauté' mode and add olive oil. Once heated, add diced onion and garlic, sautéing until translucent.
2. Add the turmeric, cumin, coriander, garam masala, mung beans, and vegetable broth to the pot. Stir to combine.
3. Add the diced carrot, bell pepper, zucchini, and tomatoes to the mixture, stirring gently.
4. Close the Instant Pot lid, set to 'Pressure Cook' or 'Manual' for 20 minutes.
5. Once cooking is complete, allow a natural pressure release. Stir in lemon juice, adjust seasonings if needed, and serve with a garnish of fresh cilantro.

Nutritional Information: 260 calories, 15g protein, 48g carbohydrates, 2g fat, 10g fiber, 0mg cholesterol, 160mg sodium, 820mg potassium.

Chickpea & Tomato Cassoulet

Yield: 4 servings | Prep time: 15 minutes | Cook time: 25 minutes

Ingredients:

- 2 cups chickpeas, soaked overnight and drained
- 3 cups low-sodium vegetable broth
- 1 onion, diced
- 3 cloves garlic, minced
- 2 cups diced tomatoes (fresh or canned without salt)
- 1 teaspoon olive oil
- 1/4 teaspoon dried thyme
- 1/4 teaspoon dried rosemary
- 1 bay leaf
- Salt and pepper to taste (use sparingly for DASH diet suitability)
- 2 tablespoons fresh parsley, chopped
- 1/2 teaspoon smoked paprika
- 1/4 cup whole wheat breadcrumbs (optional for topping)

Directions:

1. Set the Instant Pot to 'Sauté' mode and add olive oil. Once heated, add diced onion and garlic, sautéing until translucent.
2. Add chickpeas, tomatoes, thyme, rosemary, bay leaf, smoked paprika, and vegetable broth to the pot. Stir to combine.
3. Close the Instant Pot lid, set to 'Pressure Cook' or 'Manual' for 20 minutes.
4. Once cooking is complete, allow a natural pressure release. Adjust seasonings if needed, sprinkle with breadcrumbs if using, and garnish with fresh parsley before serving.

Nutritional Information: 320 calories, 16g protein, 58g carbohydrates, 4g fat, 14g fiber, 0mg cholesterol, 170mg sodium, 820mg potassium.

Pinto Bean & Roasted Pepper Salad

Yield: 4 servings | Prep time: 15 minutes | Cook time: 30 minutes

Ingredients:

- 1 cup dried pinto beans, soaked overnight and drained
- 3 cups water
- 2 large bell peppers (red and yellow), seeded and halved
- 1 medium-sized red onion, thinly sliced
- 2 cloves garlic, minced
- 2 tablespoons olive oil
- Juice of 1 lemon
- 1/4 cup fresh cilantro, chopped
- Salt and pepper to taste (use sparingly for DASH diet suitability)
- 1 teaspoon cumin (optional for added flavor)

Directions:

1. Add the soaked pinto beans and water to the Instant Pot. Secure the lid and set to 'Pressure Cook' or 'Manual' for 25 minutes. Once done, allow a natural pressure release and drain any excess water.
2. While the beans are cooking, brush the peppers with a little olive oil and place them under a broiler or on a grill, skin side up, until the skins are charred. Once charred, place them in a plastic bag for 10 minutes. This will make peeling easier. Peel off the skins and slice into thin strips.
3. In a large bowl, combine beans, roasted peppers, red onion, garlic, lemon juice, olive oil, cilantro, and cumin if using. Toss everything together, then season with salt and pepper to taste.
4. Let the salad sit for at least 10 minutes to allow flavors to meld before serving.

Nutritional Information: 280 calories, 14g protein, 40g carbohydrates, 7g fat, 10g fiber, 0mg cholesterol, 90mg sodium, 750mg potassium.

Lentil & Vegetable Minestrone

Yield: 4 servings | Prep time: 20 minutes | Cook time: 30 minutes

Ingredients:

- 1 cup dried green lentils, rinsed and drained
- 4 cups low-sodium vegetable broth
- 2 cups water
- 1 medium onion, diced
- 2 carrots, peeled and diced
- 2 celery stalks, diced
- 3 cloves garlic, minced
- 1 cup chopped tomatoes (canned or fresh)
- 1 cup chopped zucchini
- 2 cups chopped kale or spinach
- 1 teaspoon dried basil
- 1 teaspoon dried oregano
- Salt and pepper to taste (use sparingly for DASH diet suitability)
- 1 tablespoon olive oil
- 1/2 cup whole grain pasta (like small macaroni or ditalini)

Directions:

1. Set the Instant Pot to 'Sauté' mode. Add olive oil, onions, carrots, and celery. Sauté until onions are translucent, about 5 minutes.
2. Add garlic, dried basil, and oregano, and sauté for another minute.
3. Add lentils, chopped tomatoes, vegetable broth, and water to the pot. Secure the lid and set to 'Pressure Cook' or 'Manual' for 20 minutes.
4. Once done, quick-release the pressure. Add zucchini and pasta. Set the Instant Pot back to 'Sauté' mode and cook until pasta is tender, about 8-10 minutes.
5. Stir in the kale or spinach, allowing it to wilt from the heat of the soup. Season with salt and pepper to taste.

Nutritional Information: 260 calories, 15g protein, 45g carbohydrates, 3g fat, 12g fiber, 0mg cholesterol, 150mg sodium, 820mg potassium.

Decadent DASH Desserts

Berry Crumble

Yield: 4 servings | Prep time: 10 minutes | Cook time: 25 minutes

Ingredients:

- 3 cups mixed berries (like raspberries, blueberries, strawberries)
- 2 tablespoons honey or maple syrup (for a more natural sweetener)
- 1 teaspoon vanilla extract
- 1/2 cup old-fashioned rolled oats
- 1/4 cup whole wheat flour
- 2 tablespoons unsalted butter, cold and diced
- A pinch of salt
- 1/4 teaspoon ground cinnamon

Directions:

1. In a mixing bowl, combine the mixed berries with honey and vanilla extract. Transfer the mixture to the Instant Pot.
2. In another bowl, combine rolled oats, whole wheat flour, cold butter, salt, and cinnamon. Mix with your fingers until the mixture resembles coarse crumbs.
3. Sprinkle the oat mixture over the berries in the Instant Pot.
4. Secure the Instant Pot lid, set the vent to 'Sealing', and cook on 'Slow Cook' setting for 25 minutes.
5. Once done, allow it to cool for a few minutes before serving.

Nutritional Information: 210 calories, 3g protein, 38g carbohydrates, 6g fat, 5g fiber, 15mg cholesterol, 60mg sodium, 150mg potassium.

Chocolate Lava Cake

Yield: 4 servings | Prep time: 15 minutes | Cook time: 9 minutes

Ingredients:

- 1/2 cup semisweet chocolate chips (or dark chocolate with 70% cocoa content)
- 1/4 cup unsalted butter
- 1/4 cup whole wheat pastry flour
- 1/2 cup powdered sugar
- 1/8 teaspoon salt
- 1 teaspoon vanilla extract
- 2 large eggs
- 2 egg yolks

Directions:

1. In a microwave-safe bowl, melt chocolate chips and butter, stirring every 20 seconds until smooth.
2. Stir in powdered sugar, whole wheat pastry flour, salt, and vanilla extract. Once combined, whisk in eggs and egg yolks until smooth.
3. Divide batter among four greased ramekins. Place trivet into the Instant Pot and add 1 cup of water. Position the ramekins on the trivet.
4. Secure the Instant Pot lid, set the vent to 'Sealing', and select 'Manual' or 'Pressure Cook' on high pressure for 9 minutes. Once done, quick release the pressure.
5. Carefully remove the ramekins, let them cool for a minute, and serve immediately.

Nutritional Information: 275 calories, 6g protein, 28g carbohydrates, 17g fat, 2g fiber, 190mg cholesterol, 80mg sodium, 120mg potassium.

Caramelized Banana Pudding

Yield: 4 servings | Prep time: 10 minutes | Cook time: 15 minutes

Ingredients:

- 2 ripe bananas, sliced
- 1 tablespoon honey (or maple syrup for vegan version)
- 2 cups unsweetened almond milk
- 1/4 cup chia seeds

- 1 teaspoon vanilla extract
- 1/4 teaspoon cinnamon
- Pinch of salt
- Optional toppings: nuts, berries, or a sprinkle of shredded coconut

Directions:

1. Set the Instant Pot to "Sauté" mode. Add sliced bananas and honey. Cook, stirring frequently, until bananas are caramelized, approximately 3-4 minutes. Turn off the Instant Pot.
2. In a separate bowl, mix almond milk, chia seeds, vanilla extract, cinnamon, and salt. Pour this mixture over the caramelized bananas in the pot.
3. Close the Instant Pot lid, set the vent to 'Sealing', and select 'Manual' or 'Pressure Cook' on low pressure for 10 minutes. Once done, allow a natural pressure release for 5 minutes followed by a quick release.
4. Stir the pudding well. Spoon into individual bowls, garnish with optional toppings if desired, and serve either warm or chilled.

Nutritional Information: 190 calories, 5g protein, 32g carbohydrates, 6g fat, 8g fiber, 0mg cholesterol, 95mg sodium, 320mg potassium.

Peach & Almond Cobbler

Yield: 4 servings | Prep time: 15 minutes | Cook time: 25 minutes

Ingredients:

- 4 ripe peaches, pitted and sliced
- 1/4 cup honey (or maple syrup)
- 3/4 cup almond flour
- 1/4 cup unsweetened almond milk
- 2 teaspoons vanilla extract

- 1/2 teaspoon almond extract
- 1 teaspoon baking powder
- Pinch of salt
- 1/4 cup sliced almonds for topping
- 1/2 cup water (for the Instant Pot)

Directions:

1. In a mixing bowl, combine peaches and honey. Transfer the mixture to a greased oven-safe dish that fits inside your Instant Pot.
2. In another bowl, mix almond flour, almond milk, vanilla extract, almond extract, baking powder, and salt until a batter forms. Spread this batter over the peaches.
3. Sprinkle sliced almonds on top. Cover the dish with aluminum foil.
4. Pour water into the Instant Pot and place the trivet inside. Carefully set the dish on the trivet. Secure the Instant Pot lid, set the vent to 'Sealing', and select 'Manual' or 'Pressure Cook' on high pressure for 25 minutes. Allow a natural pressure release for 10 minutes after cooking, then release any remaining pressure.
5. Carefully remove the dish, uncover, and let the cobbler cool for a few minutes before serving.

Nutritional Information: 240 calories, 6g protein, 28g carbohydrates, 13g fat, 4g fiber, 0mg cholesterol, 90mg sodium, 350mg potassium.

Chocolate Quinoa Pudding

Yield: 4 servings | Prep time: 10 minutes | Cook time: 20 minutes

Ingredients:

- 1 cup quinoa, rinsed and drained
- 2 cups unsweetened almond milk
- 3 tablespoons unsweetened cocoa powder
- 1/4 cup pure maple syrup or honey
- 1 teaspoon vanilla extract
- Pinch of salt
- 1/4 cup dark chocolate chips (optional)
- Fresh berries or sliced bananas for garnish (optional)

Directions:

1. Combine quinoa, almond milk, cocoa powder, maple syrup, vanilla extract, and a pinch of salt in the Instant Pot. Stir well.
2. Secure the lid, set the vent to 'Sealing', and select 'Manual' or 'Pressure Cook' on high pressure for 12 minutes. Once the cooking time is over, let the pressure release naturally for 10 minutes, then turn the valve to 'Venting' to release any remaining pressure.
3. Open the lid and give the pudding a good stir. If you prefer a smoother texture, you can blend part or all of the mixture until creamy.
4. Stir in dark chocolate chips if using, until melted. The residual heat will melt them.
5. Serve warm or chilled, garnished with fresh berries or banana slices.

Nutritional Information: 260 calories, 8g protein, 45g carbohydrates, 6g fat, 5g fiber, 0mg cholesterol, 90mg sodium, 320mg potassium.

Vanilla Poached Pears

Yield: 4 servings | Prep time: 10 minutes | Cook time: 8 minutes

Ingredients:

- 4 medium-sized firm pears (e.g., Bosc or Anjou), peeled, halved, and cored
- 2 cups water
- 1/4 cup honey or maple syrup
- 1 vanilla bean, split lengthwise (or 1 teaspoon pure vanilla extract)
- Zest and juice of 1 lemon
- A pinch of ground cinnamon (optional)

Directions:

1. In the Instant Pot, combine water, honey or maple syrup, vanilla bean (or vanilla extract), lemon zest, lemon juice, and cinnamon, if using. Stir well until the honey or syrup dissolves.
2. Gently place the pear halves into the mixture.
3. Close the Instant Pot lid, set the vent to 'Sealing', and pressure cook on high for 8 minutes.
4. Once the cooking time is done, quick release the pressure. Carefully open the lid.
5. Using a slotted spoon, transfer the pears to serving dishes. You can reduce the poaching liquid by setting the Instant Pot to 'Sauté' mode and boiling for several minutes if a thicker syrup is desired. Pour the syrup over the pears before serving.

Nutritional Information: 160 calories, 1g protein, 42g carbohydrates, 0.5g fat, 6g fiber, 0mg cholesterol, 10mg sodium, 230mg potassium.

Apple & Cinnamon Bread Pudding

Yield: 4 servings | Prep time: 15 minutes | Cook time: 25 minutes

Ingredients:

- 4 cups day-old whole wheat bread, cubed
- 2 medium apples, peeled, cored, and diced
- 2 cups low-fat milk
- 3 large eggs
- 1/3 cup honey or maple syrup

- 1 teaspoon vanilla extract
- 1 teaspoon ground cinnamon
- 1/4 teaspoon ground nutmeg
- A pinch of salt
- Non-stick cooking spray

Directions:

1. In a large mixing bowl, whisk together milk, eggs, honey or maple syrup, vanilla extract, cinnamon, nutmeg, and salt. Add the bread cubes and diced apples, ensuring they're well-coated with the mixture. Let it sit for about 10 minutes.
2. Prepare a 7-inch springform pan by lightly spraying with non-stick cooking spray. Pour the soaked bread and apple mixture into the pan.
3. Add 1 cup of water to the Instant Pot. Place a trivet inside, and carefully set the springform pan on top of the trivet.
4. Secure the Instant Pot lid, set the vent to 'Sealing', and pressure cook on high for 25 minutes. Once done, allow a natural pressure release for 10 minutes, followed by a quick release.
5. Carefully remove the springform pan from the Instant Pot. Let the bread pudding cool for a few minutes before serving.

Nutritional Information: 320 calories, 11g protein, 60g carbohydrates, 5g fat, 6g fiber, 140mg cholesterol, 220mg sodium, 350mg potassium.

Mixed Berry Compote

Yield: 4 servings | Prep time: 5 minutes | Cook time: 5 minutes

Ingredients:

- 2 cups fresh strawberries, hulled and halved
- 1 cup fresh blueberries
- 1 cup fresh raspberries
- 2 tablespoons honey or maple syrup

- Zest and juice of 1 lemon
- 1/4 cup water
- 1 teaspoon vanilla extract
- A pinch of salt

Directions:

1. In the Instant Pot, combine strawberries, blueberries, raspberries, honey or maple syrup, lemon zest, lemon juice, water, vanilla extract, and salt.
2. Close the Instant Pot lid, set the vent to 'Sealing', and select the 'Manual' or 'Pressure Cook' function. Set it to cook on high pressure for 5 minutes.
3. Once done, allow a quick pressure release. Remove the lid and switch the Instant Pot to the 'Sauté' function.
4. Cook the compote for an additional 3-5 minutes, stirring frequently, until it thickens to your desired consistency.
5. Transfer to a jar or container and let cool. Store in the refrigerator for up to a week.

Nutritional Information: 80 calories, 1g protein, 20g carbohydrates, 0.5g fat, 4g fiber, 0mg cholesterol, 10mg sodium, 150mg potassium.

Coconut Rice Pudding with Mango

Yield: 4 servings | Prep time: 10 minutes | Cook time: 20 minutes

Ingredients:

- 1 cup Arborio rice, rinsed and drained
- 1 1/2 cups lite coconut milk
- 1 1/2 cups water
- 1/4 cup honey or maple syrup (adjust to taste)
- 1 teaspoon vanilla extract
- A pinch of salt
- 1 ripe mango, peeled, pitted, and diced
- Zest of 1 lime (for garnish)

Directions:

1. In the Instant Pot, combine the Arborio rice, coconut milk, water, honey or maple syrup, vanilla extract, and a pinch of salt.
2. Secure the lid, set the vent to 'Sealing', and select the 'Manual' or 'Pressure Cook' function. Cook on high pressure for 10 minutes.
3. Allow a natural pressure release for 10 minutes, then release any remaining pressure manually.
4. Stir the rice pudding, ensuring it has a creamy texture. If it's too thick, you can add a little more coconut milk or water to reach your desired consistency.
5. Serve in bowls, topped with diced mango and a sprinkle of lime zest.

Nutritional Information: 260 calories, 4g protein, 52g carbohydrates, 4g fat, 2g fiber, 0mg cholesterol, 50mg sodium, 200mg potassium.

Pumpkin Pie

Yield: 6 servings | Prep time: 15 minutes | Cook time: 50 minutes

Ingredients:

- 1 1/2 cups pumpkin puree (not pumpkin pie filling)
- 1/2 cup unsweetened almond milk or low-fat milk
- 2 large eggs
- 1/4 cup maple syrup or honey
- 1 teaspoon vanilla extract
- 1 1/2 teaspoons pumpkin pie spice
- 1/4 teaspoon salt
- 1 (9-inch) whole wheat pie crust (store-bought or homemade, but ensure it's DASH friendly)

Directions:

1. In a mixing bowl, whisk together pumpkin puree, almond milk, eggs, maple syrup, vanilla extract, pumpkin pie spice, and salt until well combined.
2. Pour the mixture into the whole wheat pie crust.
3. Pour 1 cup of water into the bottom of your Instant Pot and place the trivet inside. Carefully place the pie on top of the trivet.
4. Close the lid, set the Instant Pot to 'Manual' or 'Pressure Cook' and adjust to high pressure for 50 minutes. Once the cooking cycle is complete, let it naturally release for 15 minutes, then quick release the remaining pressure.
5. Carefully remove the pie and allow it to cool to room temperature. Once cooled, refrigerate for a few hours before serving.

Nutritional Information: 220 calories, 5g protein, 40g carbohydrates, 4g fat, 3g fiber, 60mg cholesterol, 150mg sodium, 250mg potassium.

Lemon & Lavender Cake

Yield: 6 servings | Prep time: 20 minutes | Cook time: 40 minutes

Ingredients:

- 1 1/2 cups whole wheat flour
- 1/2 cup almond flour
- 1 teaspoon baking powder
- 1/4 teaspoon salt
- 3/4 cup honey or maple syrup
- 1/3 cup unsweetened almond milk or low-fat milk
- 1/4 cup olive oil or melted coconut oil
- Zest and juice of 2 lemons
- 2 large eggs
- 2 teaspoons dried culinary lavender (finely chopped)

Directions:

1. In a large bowl, whisk together the whole wheat flour, almond flour, baking powder, and salt. In a separate bowl, combine honey, almond milk, oil, lemon zest, lemon juice, and eggs. Mix wet ingredients into dry ingredients until just combined. Gently fold in the lavender.
2. Pour the batter into a greased 7-inch springform pan that fits inside your Instant Pot.
3. Add 1 cup of water to the Instant Pot and place the trivet inside. Place the springform pan on the trivet.
4. Seal the Instant Pot and set to 'Manual' or 'Pressure Cook' on high for 40 minutes. Once finished, allow a natural release for 10 minutes, then do a quick release. Remove the cake, let it cool, and then transfer to a serving plate.

Nutritional Information: 270 calories, 6g protein, 45g carbohydrates, 9g fat, 4g fiber, 55mg cholesterol, 120mg sodium, 180mg potassium.

Dark Chocolate & Almond Clusters

Yield: 6 servings | Prep time: 10 minutes | Cook time: 5 minutes

Ingredients:

- 8 oz dark chocolate (at least 70% cacao)
- 1 cup unsalted almonds, whole
- 1/2 teaspoon vanilla extract
- A pinch of sea salt
- 1 tablespoon unsweetened shredded coconut (optional)

Directions:

1. Break the dark chocolate into smaller pieces and place them in a heatproof bowl that fits into the Instant Pot.
2. Fill the Instant Pot with 1 cup of water and place the trivet at the bottom. Place the bowl with chocolate on the trivet.
3. Set the Instant Pot to the 'Saute' mode and melt the chocolate, stirring occasionally. This should take about 3-5 minutes.
4. Once the chocolate is melted, stir in the vanilla extract, almonds, and sea salt until the almonds are well coated.
5. Using a spoon, scoop out clusters of almonds coated with chocolate and place them on a parchment-lined tray or plate. Optionally, sprinkle with shredded coconut. Allow to cool and solidify before serving.

Nutritional Information: 210 calories, 5g protein, 15g carbohydrates, 16g fat, 4g fiber, 0mg cholesterol, 5mg sodium, 230mg potassium.

Strawberry & Rhubarb Crisp

Yield: 4 servings | Prep time: 15 minutes | Cook time: 20 minutes

Ingredients:

- 1 cup strawberries, hulled and halved
- 1 cup rhubarb, chopped into 1/2-inch pieces
- 1/4 cup honey or maple syrup
- 1 teaspoon vanilla extract
- 1/2 cup old-fashioned rolled oats
- 2 tablespoons whole wheat flour
- 2 tablespoons unsalted butter, cold and cut into small pieces
- A pinch of salt
- 1/4 teaspoon ground cinnamon

Directions:

1. In a mixing bowl, combine strawberries, rhubarb, half of the honey or maple syrup, and vanilla extract. Mix well and transfer to a heatproof dish that fits into the Instant Pot.
2. In another bowl, mix the oats, whole wheat flour, remaining honey or maple syrup, butter, salt, and cinnamon. Use your fingers to mix until the mixture is crumbly.
3. Spread the oat mixture over the strawberry and rhubarb mixture.
4. Add 1 cup of water to the Instant Pot and place the trivet inside. Place the dish on the trivet. Close the lid and set the Instant Pot to 'Manual' or 'Pressure Cook' mode and cook for 20 minutes.
5. Once done, do a quick release and carefully remove the dish. Allow the crisp to cool slightly before serving.

Nutritional Information:220 calories, 3g protein, 40g carbohydrates, 6g fat, 4g fiber, 15mg cholesterol, 55mg sodium, 350mg potassium.

Pineapple Upside-Down Cake

Yield: 4 servings | Prep time: 20 minutes | Cook time: 35 minutes

Ingredients:

- 4 pineapple slices
- 8 maraschino cherries
- 1/3 cup honey or maple syrup, divided
- 1 cup whole wheat pastry flour
- 1 teaspoon baking powder
- 1/4 teaspoon baking soda
- Pinch of salt
- 1/4 cup unsweetened applesauce
- 1 large egg
- 1 teaspoon vanilla extract
- 1/2 cup low-fat milk or almond milk

Directions:

1. In a heatproof round cake pan that fits into the Instant Pot, arrange pineapple slices at the bottom. Place a maraschino cherry in the center of each pineapple slice and in between, if desired. Drizzle with half of the honey or maple syrup.
2. In a mixing bowl, combine flour, baking powder, baking soda, and salt. In another bowl, whisk together applesauce, egg, vanilla extract, milk, and the remaining honey or maple syrup. Pour the wet ingredients into the dry ingredients and mix until just combined.
3. Pour the batter over the pineapple slices in the cake pan.
4. Add 1 cup of water to the Instant Pot and place the trivet inside. Place the cake pan on the trivet. Close the lid, set the Instant Pot to 'Manual' or 'Pressure Cook' mode, and cook for 35 minutes.
5. Once done, do a quick release and carefully remove the cake pan. Allow the cake to cool slightly, then invert onto a plate, so the pineapple slices are on top.

Nutritional Information:280 calories, 5g protein, 58g carbohydrates, 3g fat, 4g fiber, 45mg cholesterol, 230mg sodium, 230mg potassium.

Creamy Lemon & Berry Parfait

Yield: 4 servings | Prep time: 15 minutes | Cook time: 8 minutes

Ingredients:

- 2 cups mixed berries (blueberries, raspberries, strawberries, etc.)
- 2 tbsp honey or maple syrup
- Zest and juice of 1 lemon
- 1 cup low-fat Greek yogurt
- 1/2 cup low-fat granola (no added sugar)
- 1 tsp vanilla extract
- Fresh mint leaves for garnish (optional)

Directions:

1. In the Instant Pot, combine mixed berries, half the lemon zest, lemon juice, and honey or maple syrup. Gently stir to combine.
2. Close the Instant Pot lid, set the valve to sealing, and set it on 'Manual' or 'Pressure Cook' mode for 3 minutes.
3. Once done, perform a quick release and transfer the berry mixture to a bowl. Allow it to cool.
4. In another bowl, mix Greek yogurt with vanilla extract and the remaining lemon zest.
5. Assemble the parfait in glasses or jars by layering yogurt, berry mixture, and granola. Repeat layers until all ingredients are used up. Garnish with fresh mint leaves if desired.

Nutritional Information: 190 calories, 10g protein, 28g carbohydrates, 3g fat, 3g fiber, 5mg cholesterol, 40mg sodium, 180mg potassium.

Festive DASH Feasts for Special Occasions

Herb-Infused Turkey with Cranberry Sauce

Yield: 4 servings | Prep time: 20 minutes | Cook time: 40 minutes

Ingredients:

- 4 turkey breasts (boneless, skinless)
- 1 tbsp olive oil
- 1 tsp dried rosemary
- 1 tsp dried thyme
- 1 tsp dried sage
- 1/4 cup low-sodium chicken broth
- 1 cup fresh cranberries
- 2 tbsp honey or maple syrup
- Zest and juice of 1 orange
- Salt and pepper to taste (use sparingly)

Directions:

1. Season the turkey breasts with rosemary, thyme, sage, salt, and pepper. Turn on the Instant Pot on 'Sauté' mode and add olive oil. Brown the turkey breasts for about 2-3 minutes on each side.
2. Add chicken broth to the pot. Close the lid, set the valve to sealing, and pressure cook on high for 25 minutes.
3. In a separate saucepan over medium heat, combine cranberries, honey or maple syrup, orange zest, and juice. Simmer until cranberries burst and sauce thickens, about 15 minutes.
4. Once the Instant Pot cycle is done, wait for natural pressure release, then open the lid.
5. Serve the turkey breasts with a generous spoonful of cranberry sauce on top.

Nutritional Information: 310 calories, 40g protein, 18g carbohydrates, 8g fat, 2g fiber, 85mg cholesterol, 70mg sodium, 550mg potassium.

Garlic & Herb Roast Beef

Yield: 4 servings | Prep time: 15 minutes | Cook time: 60 minutes

Ingredients:

- 2 lbs beef roast (choose a lean cut)
- 4 garlic cloves, minced
- 1 tbsp dried rosemary
- 1 tbsp dried thyme
- 1 cup low-sodium beef broth
- 1 tbsp olive oil
- Salt and pepper to taste (use sparingly)
- 1 bay leaf

Directions:

1. In a small bowl, mix together minced garlic, rosemary, thyme, salt, and pepper. Rub this mixture all over the beef roast.
2. Turn the Instant Pot to 'Sauté' mode and add olive oil. Brown the roast on all sides, roughly 3-4 minutes per side.
3. Pour in the low-sodium beef broth and add the bay leaf.
4. Close the Instant Pot lid, set the valve to sealing, and set it to 'Meat/Stew' mode or 'Manual/Pressure Cook' on high for 50 minutes.
5. Once the cycle completes, allow for a natural pressure release. Remove the beef, slice, and serve.

Nutritional Information: 340 calories, 48g protein, 3g carbohydrates, 15g fat, 0.5g fiber, 120mg cholesterol, 180mg sodium, 620mg potassium.

Citrus-Herb Brined Chicken

Yield: 4 servings | Prep time: 120 minutes (including brining time) | Cook time: 25 minutes

Ingredients:

- 4 boneless, skinless chicken breasts
- 2 cups low-sodium chicken broth
- Juice and zest of 1 lemon
- Juice and zest of 1 orange
- 1 tbsp olive oil

- 2 garlic cloves, minced
- 2 tsp rosemary, finely chopped
- 2 tsp thyme, finely chopped
- Salt and pepper to taste (use sparingly)

Brine:

1. In a large bowl, combine low-sodium chicken broth, lemon and orange juice, and zest. Add garlic, rosemary, thyme, salt, and pepper. Submerge chicken breasts in the mixture and refrigerate for 2 hours.

Directions:

1. After brining, remove chicken breasts from the liquid and pat dry with paper towels.
2. Turn on the Instant Pot to 'Sauté' mode and add olive oil. Brown the chicken breasts on both sides, roughly 2-3 minutes per side.
3. Pour in 1 cup of the brining liquid into the Instant Pot.
4. Close the Instant Pot lid, set the valve to sealing, and set to 'Poultry' mode or 'Manual/Pressure Cook' on high for 20 minutes.
5. Once the cycle completes, allow for a natural pressure release. Remove chicken and serve.

Nutritional Information: 210 calories, 30g protein, 5g carbohydrates, 6g fat, 1g fiber, 75mg cholesterol, 200mg sodium, 500mg potassium.

Stuffed Pork Loin with Apricots & Walnuts

Yield: 4 servings | Prep time: 20 minutes | Cook time: 45 minutes

Ingredients:

- 1 pork loin (about 2 pounds)
- 1/2 cup dried apricots, finely chopped
- 1/4 cup walnuts, finely chopped
- 1 tbsp fresh rosemary, minced

- 2 garlic cloves, minced
- 1 cup low-sodium chicken broth
- 1 tbsp olive oil
- Salt and pepper to taste (use sparingly)

Directions:

1. In a medium-sized bowl, combine chopped apricots, walnuts, rosemary, and minced garlic. Mix well.
2. Butterfly the pork loin and season the inside with a pinch of salt and pepper. Spread the apricot and walnut mixture on the inside of the pork loin. Roll up the pork loin and secure with butcher's twine.
3. Turn on the Instant Pot to 'Sauté' mode and add olive oil. Brown the pork loin on all sides, roughly 4-5 minutes per side.
4. Pour in the low-sodium chicken broth. Close the Instant Pot lid, set the valve to sealing, and set to 'Manual/Pressure Cook' on high for 40 minutes.
5. Once the cycle completes, allow for a natural pressure release for 10 minutes, then quick release the remaining pressure. Remove pork loin, let it rest for a few minutes, slice, and serve.

Nutritional Information: 380 calories, 45g protein, 18g carbohydrates, 12g fat, 2g fiber, 120mg cholesterol, 190mg sodium, 600mg potassium.

Seafood Bouillabaisse for the Holidays

Yield: 4 servings | Prep time: 15 minutes | Cook time: 30 minutes

Ingredients:

- 1/2 pound fresh cod, cut into chunks
- 1/2 pound fresh shrimp, peeled and deveined
- 1/4 pound fresh mussels, cleaned and de-bearded
- 1/4 pound fresh clams, cleaned
- 1 onion, finely chopped
- 3 cloves garlic, minced
- 1 can (14 oz) low-sodium diced tomatoes
- 2 cups low-sodium vegetable broth
- 1/4 cup white wine (optional)
- 1 tsp olive oil
- 1 tsp fresh thyme, chopped
- 1 tsp fresh parsley, chopped
- 1 bay leaf
- Zest of 1 orange
- Salt and pepper to taste (use sparingly)

Directions:

1. Set Instant Pot to 'Sauté' mode. Add olive oil, onion, and garlic. Sauté until onion is translucent.
2. Add white wine (if using) to deglaze the pot. Stir well.
3. Add diced tomatoes, vegetable broth, thyme, parsley, bay leaf, and orange zest. Stir to combine.
4. Add cod, shrimp, mussels, and clams. Close the lid and set the Instant Pot to 'Soup' mode for 20 minutes.
5. Once done, allow for a natural pressure release for 5 minutes, then release the remaining pressure. Carefully open the lid, discard the bay leaf, and season with a pinch of salt and pepper if desired. Serve hot with a sprinkle of fresh parsley.

Nutritional Information: 280 calories, 34g protein, 15g carbohydrates, 7g fat, 3g fiber, 90mg cholesterol, 320mg sodium, 650mg potassium.

Honey & Mustard Glazed Ham

Yield: 4 servings | Prep time: 10 minutes | Cook time: 25 minutes

Ingredients:

- 2 pounds boneless ham, low-sodium
- 1/4 cup honey
- 2 tablespoons Dijon mustard, low-sodium
- 1/2 cup pineapple juice
- 1 clove garlic, minced
- 1/4 teaspoon ground black pepper
- 1/4 teaspoon ground cloves
- 1 cup water

Directions:

1. In a bowl, mix together honey, Dijon mustard, garlic, black pepper, and cloves to create the glaze.
2. Pour water and pineapple juice into the Instant Pot. Place the trivet in the pot and then place the ham on top of the trivet.
3. Brush a generous amount of the honey-mustard glaze over the ham.
4. Close the Instant Pot lid, set it to "Manual" or "Pressure Cook" on high pressure for 25 minutes. Once done, allow for a natural pressure release for 10 minutes, then release any remaining pressure.
5. Once opened, brush the ham with the remaining glaze and let it sit for a few minutes before slicing. Serve warm.

Nutritional Information: 320 calories, 28g protein, 20g carbohydrates, 14g fat, 0g fiber, 85mg cholesterol, 850mg sodium, 420mg potassium.

Vegetable & Nut Wellington

Yield: 4 servings | Prep time: 20 minutes | Cook time: 25 minutes

Ingredients:

- 1 sheet of whole wheat puff pastry, thawed
- 1 tablespoon olive oil
- 1 medium onion, diced
- 2 cloves garlic, minced
- 1 cup mushrooms, finely chopped
- 1/2 cup carrots, finely chopped
- 1/2 cup red bell pepper, finely chopped
- 1 cup mixed nuts (e.g., walnuts, pecans, and almonds), coarsely chopped
- 1/4 cup fresh parsley, chopped
- 1 tablespoon soy sauce, low sodium
- 1/2 teaspoon black pepper
- 1 cup vegetable broth, low sodium
- 1 tablespoon cornstarch

Directions:

1. Turn on the Instant Pot to "Sauté" mode. Heat olive oil and sauté onion and garlic until translucent. Add mushrooms, carrots, and bell peppers, cooking until softened.
2. Add the mixed nuts, parsley, soy sauce, and black pepper, stirring well. Dissolve cornstarch in vegetable broth and pour into the mixture. Continue to stir until the mixture thickens.
3. Turn off the Instant Pot. Let the vegetable and nut mixture cool.
4. Roll out the puff pastry and place the cooled mixture in the center. Fold the pastry over the mixture and seal the edges to form the Wellington. Use the Instant Pot's steam function and cook for 20 minutes.
5. Once done, allow the Wellington to sit for a few minutes before slicing. Serve warm.

Nutritional Information: 450 calories, 12g protein, 45g carbohydrates, 27g fat, 7g fiber, 0mg cholesterol, 280mg sodium, 500mg potassium.

Made in the USA
Las Vegas, NV
29 September 2023

78298233R00046